WHAT IF?

Learning For the Twenty First Century

Jeff McMillan

1st WORLD
PUBLISHING

What If?

Learning For the Twenty First Century

Jeff McMillan

© Jeff McMillan 2010

Published by 1stWorld Publishing
P.O. Box 2211, Fairfield, Iowa 52556
tel: 641-209-5000 • fax: 866-440-5234
web: www.1stworldpublishing.com

First Edition

LCCN: 2010935115
SoftCover ISBN: 978-1-4218-9168-2
HardCover ISBN: 978-1-4218-9169-9
eBook ISBN: 978-1-4218-9170-5

To my adventurous daughter, Jennifer, who inspires me to make a difference.

To Rich, my friend, colleague and first mate on this wonderful journey of discovery.

To Olga, our leader who guided us through rough water as we sailed the high seas.

Table of Contents

Preface

Get REEL: Relevant, Engaging, Enduring, Learning

Nothing fosters learning more than an internal passion for a subject. Once the fire has been lit, and the engagement begins, there is no stopping the imagination or the depth of understanding. The ultimate goal of education should be to light the fire in each child's soul and to create an endless thirst for knowledge and truth. We should be helping our students develop skills to become life-long learners, confident in their ability to communicate and collaborate, and creative in the way they solve problems.

Schools and school districts throughout North America, and around the world, are searching for ways of keeping young people interested and engaged in their learning. Students are dropping out, both figuratively and literally, in alarming numbers. Professional educators grapple with strategies to increase the graduation rate of students and are constantly looking at "new" methods that will keep students interested in learning. Our knowledge of how students learn, gives us a clear understanding of the type of teaching that should be used to engage learning and improve cognitive development. Educators must be aware of the needs and interests of our students. The students must see how learning connects to the world beyond the walls of the school. To fully engage learners, it is important to make it "real". Young people enjoy the feeling of being a part of the adult world, making adult decisions.

They want to know that what they are learning has real world applications.

Several years ago I was given the opportunity to create a program that would take students to new heights of engagement. In partnership with a colleague, under the careful guidance of our administrator, and with the support of our supervisory officers, we set off to discover the art of engaging students. First, we explored existing programs that were designed to develop advanced learning, through experiential education. We immediately witnessed the benefits of this approach. We noticed the reactions of the students to this style of teaching and were amazed at the sense of ownership they shared. We agreed, that to truly engage our students in the learning process, we had to create a program that was meaningful, reality-based and which catered to the specific needs and learning styles of our student population.

It was at this point that the process of creating The Current Experience began. The original title was selected to reflect current knowledge and understanding of student learning. We wanted the strategies to be experiential and therefore the word experience was chosen as part of the title. Our mission was to develop a program that was relevant to the students, one that would address their individual differences, while helping them develop the skills to become life-long learners. As a team, we developed an environment that was creative, engaging and motivating. An integrated course of study was designed to develop knowledge and understanding. We wanted the learning to be enduring and transferrable, while directly connected to the existing curriculum. We created a plan for the delivery of the program and carefully researched, and implemented, effective assessment strategies that would help our students move forward as learners. Students were taught to reflect on their learning experiences through the use of metacognitive activities and journal entries. What we learned throughout the next few years, lead to the creation of the Get REEL approach to learning.

We were determined to use sound teaching practices that would motivate, engage and prompt our students to learn. The Current Experience included teaching a balanced, integrated curriculum. It was designed to meet the individual needs of all learners, while providing active, relevant opportunities for the students to internalize their learning. Careful attention was given to global and cultural awareness. Creativity, critical thinking and problem solving became the cornerstone for many activities and explorations. Technology was encouraged to be used, as a tool for the enhancement of learning and for demonstrating understanding. Allowing the students to become personally involved in learning experiences, provided the intrinsic motivation for engagement. The learners felt empowered and in control of their learning. Self and peer evaluation was ongoing and became a critical part of the growth of all students.

Our students saw us as learners and watched as our enthusiasm and excitement spread throughout the school and the school district. It became the most rewarding experience of my 30 years of teaching and energized all of us involved, students, teachers and administration. Never, as teachers, had we worked harder and never had we seen such positive results in students. The energy that was created by our teaching was so much more than we had ever imagined and we strongly believed that there was no better way to teach. We had struck the mother lode and our students were rich beyond their dreams. Not only had we lit a fire in the hearts of our students, we also lit a fire in our souls.

I was a teacher for 30 years. I experienced a successful and exciting career, filled with a life time of smiles and memories. From the moment I stood in front of my first class, to the last bell before my retirement, I never stopped learning. This book is a continuation of my journey. It is food for my soul, the water that helps quench my thirst for understanding and truth. I had to find an explanation for the success of Get REEL. It was a magical experience. We knew that what we were exploring, and the great accomplishments we were seeing, had to have a theoretical foundation. To us it was common sense, supported by solid research and backed by reliable data. In writing this book, I am showing the rationale behind our success and in doing so encouraging others to think outside the box. Many times, we were asked by teachers, to explain how they could use this approach with their students. This book begins by working through the theoretical background and the information supporting Get REEL. The final chapter outlines the process involved in planning, designing and implementing the Get REEL strategies.

The first two chapters are designed to create an awareness of the need for change in the educational system. The students I taught in my last few years of teaching did not resemble the learners I was introduced to as a beginning teacher in 1977. The world around me had undergone significant changes. Technology had become a dominant force and a huge factor in change. The world was different. Our students were different and the world into which they "graduated" was very complex. As educators, we must recognize this change and come to the understanding that we must alter the way we are doing things.

Chapters three and four are devoted to creating an understanding of the need for creativity in education today. Also discussed, is the importance of global awareness, cultural understanding and the effective use of technology in schools. The walls of the world are tumbling down and with this change is the need for understanding and cooperation. Creative and collaborative solutions, to the many problems threatening our planet, must be found. The song titled, "We are the World" has taken on a deeper meaning in the global economy. Technology has brought us closer than we could ever have imagined. Our students are born "digital natives" and fully understand that the world is only a keystroke away, while information and entertainment is available on demand, 24 hours a day, 7 days a week.

Chapters five, six and seven explore the changing role of the educator and how this new role relates to the learning process. New research on the brain and cognition explains the complexity of learning. Teachers must abandon their role as "sages on the stage" and become learning coaches. Student learning involves making connections through integrated experiences and it is the responsibility of the teachers to provide these learning opportunities. The effective use of formative assessment becomes an invaluable tool in helping learners move forward in their understanding of skills and concepts. Assessment for learning becomes the guide for program development and differentiation of instruction.

Balancing the curriculum is discussed in chapter seven. Designing a productive learning environment requires alignment among four areas; student focus, thinking focus, assessment focus and team. The learning experience must reflect the needs of the student, with an emphasis on developing thinking skills. Attention to assessment strategies is vital for learning to take place. The creation of a creative, safe, learning environment provides the learners with a supportive culture for growth.

The final chapter explains the Get REEL strategies. It brings together the theories and teaching practices involved in the implementation of this style of teaching and learning. The planning model, APAA (Awareness, Passion, Audience, Action) that we developed, is discussed and examples are given to show how the program can be used. Maintaining curriculum connections is important when using the Get REEL approach and, therefore knowledge of enduring understandings and essential learning becomes critical to the planning process.

Get REEL is an exciting and highly engaging approach to teaching that meets the needs of the learners in the 21st century. I invite you to join me on my journey of discovery and strongly encourage you to move beyond your comfort zone. Step outside of the box an enjoy learning in the 21st century.

Introduction

"If we teach today as we taught yesterday, we rob our children of tomorrow."

—John Dewey

To many adults and parents, school should be a reflection of the society it serves. As teachers we often hear "that is not the way it is in the 'real' world." We are told that the world of work is a cold place where superiors care nothing about you personally and focus completely on results. Employers are not interested in your ideas and don't pat you on the back for a good effort. Blind obedience to company policy is demanded and loyalty is unquestionable. Comply or be fired!

Their real world is summarized in the following, often quoted, internet posting: Circulating via email, the text of a speech allegedly given by Bill Gates in which he sets out 11 rules of life for today's high school students. This was not spoken by Bill Gates, it's an urban legend about life beyond school. It describes how feel-good, politically correct educators have created a full generation of kids with no concept of reality and how this concept has set them up for failure in the real world

Rule 1: Life is not fair—get used to it!

Rule 2: The world won't care about your self-esteem. The world will expect you to accomplish something before you feel good about yourself.

Rule 3: You will not make $60,000 a year right out of high school. You won't be a vice-president with a car phone until you earn both.

Rule 4: If you think your teacher is tough, wait till you get a boss.

Rule 5: Flipping burgers is not beneath your dignity. Your Grandparents had a different word for burger flipping—they called it opportunity.

Rule 6: If you mess up, it's not your parents' fault, so don't whine about your mistakes, learn from them.

Rule 7: Before you were born, your parents weren't as boring as they are now. They got that way from paying your bills, cleaning your clothes and listening to you talk about how cool you thought you are. So before you save the rain forest from the parasites of your parent's generation, try delousing the closet in your own room.

Rule 8: Your school may have done away with winners and losers, but life has not. In some schools they have abolished failing grades and they'll give you as many times as you want to get the right answer. This doesn't bear the slightest resemblance to anything in real life.

Rule 9: Life is not divided into semesters. You don't get summers off and very few employers are interested in helping you find yourself. Do that on your own time.

Rule 10: Television is not real life. In real life people actually have to leave the coffee shop and go to jobs.

Rule 11: Be nice to nerds. Chances are you'll end up working for one.

To think that we must prepare our students for the realities of the "real" world is a bad decision. Companies that work under the outdated industrial model of employer—employee relationships are plagued by workers who lack job satisfaction, who are frequently absent from work and display total lack of commitment and company loyalty. What if society became a reflection of schools where instead of blind obedience and fear of disciplinary measures we had a work culture built on respect, acceptance, commitment, sharing of ideas, cooperation, collaboration, creative problem solving and critical thinking, work culture that promoted individual growth and rewarded workers for their engagement?

Rework, is the new book by 37 Signals, the online tools company. There is a section called 'Ignore the real world'. They discuss how often they are told "That would never work in the real world". The book continues: "The real world sounds like an awfully depressing place to live. It's a place where new ideas, unfamiliar approaches and foreign concepts always lose. The only things that win are what people already know and do, even if those things are flawed and inefficient." Is this the real world they are talking about?

In 2007, Salary.com conducted a survey of nearly 12000 employees. The survey found that more than 60 percent of the workers planned on searching for a new job during the next three months. While it was shown that salary was a factor in this lack of job satisfaction, it was not necessarily the contributing factor. Many leave their jobs because they find the work unchallenging, not meaningful or that the work environment is uncaring. A 2005 study by Towers Perrin found that 86 percent of the world's employees were not prepared to go the extra mile for their employers and a poll by the Society for Human Resource Management found that three-fourths of U.S. workers were not loyal to their employers and were in fact actively looking for new employment opportunities. Gallup's poll on employee engagement shows that two-thirds to three-quarters of U.S. employees are not engaged in their work. It was discovered that this lack of commitment was not just in the lower levels of the organization but also found in the higher levels of management. Is this the "real" world we are preparing our students for?

Hudson, an international recruiting firm surveyed 10,000 workers in 2005 and released a study called "Why Employees Walk: 2005 Retention Initiative Report". They discovered that although many employees require good pay and benefits to stay on the job, when their personal needs were not met in the areas of career growth and professional development or when they felt they did not have a good working relationship with their boss, they were more likely to look for work elsewhere.

Absenteeism is defined as a failure to report to work. Its annual cost has been estimated at over $40 billion for U.S companies and $12 billion for Canadian firms. The cost of absenteeism is greater than the direct payment of wages and benefits paid during the absence. Organizations must also consider the indirect costs of staffing, scheduling, re-training, lost productivity, diminished moral, and so on. The indirect costs often exceed the direct cost of absenteeism. It is obvious that it is difficult for a company to operate smoothly under these conditions. Is this the "real" world they are talking about?

In 2008-2009 the planet was crushed by a collapse of the global financial system. Among many serious economic issues, over spending and inability to repay debts laid the foundation for a recession that rocked nations around the world. According to the U.S. Federal Reserve, consumer credit card debt now exceeds more than $750 billion. An estimated 28 million Americans are classified as "unbanked" meaning they do not have bank accounts and must rely on payday type loan establishments that charge excessive fees to survive. Many people are living so far in debt that they will never be able to recover. In 2008, 1,416,902 people in the U.S. filed for personal bankruptcy because they could no long meet their financial obligations. By the end of the fiscal year in 2009, almost 150,000 Canadians filed for personal bank-ruptcy. The trend in both U.S.A. and Canada indicates that financial failures are on the rise, meaning the situation is getting worse rather than better. Is this the "real" world they are talking about?

The President's Advisory Council on Financial Literacy Report 2008 identified financial illiteracy as among the many causes for the financial and credit crisis. According to the Jump$tart Coalition, high school students in the United States scored only 48.3% in a recent financial literacy test. The same test given to college student resulted in only slightly better score coming in at 62.2%. Today's learner must obtain a basic education in financial literacy. They need to learn about the money realities of the world both personally and globally. Attention needs to be focussed on mortgage terms and conditions, the impact of compound interest on credit card debt, diversification in investing, the value of saving, living within ones means and so on. If in addition to teaching reading and writing within our schools we teach financial literacy, we will provide today's learners with the opportunity to have a more secure financial future. Helping them develop an "economic way of thinking" by exposing them to the realities of personal spending will be good for them as individuals and us as a nation.

> "We have learned many lessons from the current economic crisis. But none is more important than this: financial literacy is critical to our economic well being, and, unfortunately, we are not making the grade."
>
> —Financial Literacy Now: New York, Business Week article 2009

In March, 2007 it was estimated that the cost of post 9/11 military operations for the United States had escalated to over $510 billion. As of July, 2009 the monthly obligations for military pay and contracts was $10.9 billion. The price of military action in Iraq, Afghanistan and other global war measures against terrorism continues to rise. The world is in a constant state of turmoil. People die over different political, philosophical and religious beliefs. Racism and bias continues to dominate the thoughts of many who refuse to accept the rights of others to be different. Cultural awareness and a global understanding and the need for cooperation and understanding is lacking on many levels. The planet, while at war with each other, is slowly dying as a result of people's demand for non-renewable resources. Global warming and the never ending need for oil has created major problems that the people of our planet must join together to solve. Is this the "real" world they are talking about?

Ah, the cold realities of the "real" world. The new global economy is demanding huge changes not only from its workers but from the companies themselves. It is now recognized by many industry giants that the old way of conducting business will not guarantee prosperity. What is becoming a corporation's largest asset are their employees. A company that looks towards the future has a fundamental goal: to constantly seek innovative solutions, in other words to be constantly generating new ideas and new strategies, with the ability to make quick accurate decisions. Today, the future of a company is not tomorrow, but the next minute. To accomplish this goal requires creative and energetic workers who have the freedom to explore ideas and are rewarded for their accomplishments through intrinsic rewards, and to a lesser degree extrinsic motivators. People are a company's greatest strength. It is a corporation's personnel, designers, technicians, engineers, sales people and front-line workers that are the driving force needed to ensure success and growth. Many companies are recognizing the importance of changing the way they engage with their workers and are developing new strategies to meet their individual needs. Keeping the brightest workers motivated is becoming an important consideration for companies in today's global economy. Companies such as Google, Westjet, IDEO and Toyota are just a few of the organizations that are paying close attention to the engagement of their workers. These highly successful businesses are on the cutting edge of what is required to maintain a competitive advantage in the 21st century.

The Directors of Google, when describing things they know to be true about company success, talk about the importance of creating the right company culture and how this culture allows great, creative things to happen. Google leaders believe that work should be challenging and the challenge should be fun. They place a huge emphasis on team achievements and take great pride in individual accomplishments. They put great stock in their employees who display energetic and passion for creative approaches to work, play and life.

Clive Beddoe, former CEO of Westjet Airlines told an audience, "We have turned our employees into capitalists...We encourage them to think like owners." Westjet hires people for their positive attitude and will train them to do the job. The successful airline company believes in trust and empowerment. Their priorities are its people first then guests followed by shareholders. It's their belief that great employees give great customer service and consistently strive to do their personal best.

IDEO is an extremely successful company that designs products, services and experiences ranging from Apples computer mouse to a patient-care delivery system at SSM DePaul Health Centre in St. Louis Missouri. Tim Brown, CEO of the design firm, attributes the success of his company to the importance of leadership and incentives for creating a culture of creativity and innovation. Brown emphasizes the need for a culture of creativity where the employees feel valued for their contributions. IDEO provides its workers with the opportunity to do things that have an impact on the world, to work on projects that they believe. IDEO employees feel personally engaged in the innovative exploration of ideas at both an individual and team level. The workers are valued for their contributions and encouraged to develop skills that will be valued by them as individuals and as members of a highly productive, energetic team.

The underlying principles that support what is known as the Toyota Way place a huge emphasis on the respect of employees. Every effort is made by the organization to understand each other and to take responsibility for building mutual trust among workers. Toyota values teamwork that stimulates personal and profession growth, creating opportunities for the development of innovative ideas and problem solving solutions. Toyota leaders want a culture that develops workers who will thoroughly understand and value the company philosophy while creating a desire to share that belief with others in the corporations. Toyota strives to create and maintain a positive culture that values the contributions of the individual, knowing that this will help create a worker that is loyal and committed to the company and to the vision of the organization.

There is change coming in the world of business. The old paradigm for company success was to keep the customer happy. The new paradigm says that the employees are a first priority and keeping them happy should be one of their main goals. Neglect their needs and they won't be around and when they go they may well take their customers with them. According to Dave Ulrich, a human resource consultant and professor at Ross School of Business at the University of Michigan, to keep employees happy, motivated and engaged, companies must take care of their employees personal needs first.

> "My colleagues and I have found that next generation leaders for any organization may be competent (able to do work) and committed (willing to do work), but unless they are making a real contribution through the work (finding mean and purpose in their work), then their interest in what they are doing diminishes and their willingness to harness their talent in the organization wanes. Contributions occur when employees feel that their personal needs are being met through participation in their organization."
>
> —Dave Ulrich

The future of our planet rests in the hands of our youth. We desperately need learners who are creative, critical thinkers, students who are accepting of other points of views and who can collaborate across boundaries to find solutions to the problems that plague our cities and nations around the world. We need citizens who are capable of making wise, informed decisions that will benefit their families and the needs of those around them. We must have people who understand what it means to learn and have the ability to learn and relearn, individuals who feel comfortable with themselves and confidant in their abilities to be active, participating members of society.

Unfortunately, none of this is possible under the present system that is used to educate our students. A huge shift in what we do and how we do it is required if we are to prepare our citizens to address the needs of the 21st century. The stakes are high and the demands are many. Change has been a very slow process in the area of education. Few, if any companies in the world today could survive if they moved at the snail pace of education. They would have been out of business years ago, smothered by those who recognized and adjusted to the needs of their consumers. The world is changing rapidly and it is imperative that institutions recognize the need to do things differently. Everyone, teachers, students, politicians and parents need to change their minds about what school is and what it can be. A paradigm explosion is required and the spark needs to be lit now.

The cry for change is not new and the causes of the failure of the system are well documented. Research continues to shed light on the need for transformation in how we teach our children. Many influential people around the world are devoting large amounts of time and money to create new schools and to advocate for school change. Yet, the system remains virtually unchanged, a system originally built over a hundred years ago to meet the needs of an industrial age where mass production and conformity were the requirements. The concept of factory-style education, where students learn in disconnected surroundings, demanding conformity over creativity, where facts predominated over meaning, where bureaucracy dominates reasoning, will not meet the demands of the citizens of tomorrow.

What if schools stopped "manufacturing" students and started to create learners who valued education? The present system is dominated by largeness; large schools, large classes, large counties or school districts. The face of education has been defined by textbook producers, testing companies, school supply businesses, school construction companies, lobby groups, politicians and so on. From this industrial model came the need for "standardized" testing to ensure product quality as the students move along the educational conveyor belt. The coldness of the production system has led to generations of learners who have been mass produced, all looking virtually the same, compliant and waiting to be told what to do by those in positions of authority.

The schools of the 21st century need to embrace the power of downsizing. More people need to come in direct contact with the learner. This implies a downsizing in the bureaucratic hierarchy of the educational system, putting power in the classroom and enabling teachers to make a difference. Putting the "human" factor into our schools will allow educators and students to engage in learning experiences that move beyond indoctrinating to empowering them to use their strengths and talents to make a positive contribution to the world around them. The more intimate the contact, the better the opportunity for understanding and growth.

What if schools were designed around small collaborative teams designed to meet the individual needs of the learner while promoting independence and freedom to explore? High schools are historically organized around a department structure that serves the needs of particular areas of study, for example the math department or history department. This model, originally used by universities in medieval Europe, continues to form the structure for the delivery of education today. This large and impersonal system where subjects are taught separately, often leads to students feeling isolated and not connected to their learning. Subject specialist, (high school teachers) may see over 150 students in a day resulting in their inability to make personal connections with the students. Many students fall through the cracks and disappear without being noticed, leading to an increase in the dropout rate. The delivery of knowledge cannot become more important than the student. Because of the industrial nature of the school system, teachers are expected to maintain conformity in curriculum, teaching methods, student behaviour and so on. Maverick teachers who "buck" the system and provide an engaging, creative, student centred learning environment are often regarded as heroes by the students and renegades by their colleagues. Creative teaching needs to become the rule rather than the exception.

> "Exceptional teachers, the ones who make a difference, are not only rare, but they're almost always in trouble for bending the rules and not optimizing for the standardized tests."
>
> —Seth Godin, Brainwashed: Seven ways to reinvent yourself

The global economy demands a new type of worker, one who is creative and self-sufficient. The need for creativity should dominate the need for conformity. Small, personalized learning environments that encourage collaboration, cultural awareness, critical thinking while providing engaging, meaningful learning experiences is a step forward in creating the type of citizen required for the 21st century.

What if our educational system was based on our new understanding of how students learn? Teachers cannot simply pour information into the heads of students and expect them to grasp the concepts. Learning is an active process through which the learner constructs meaning by making connections. These connections are enhanced when students are engaged in exploration, experimentation, discussions and personal reflection. In an age where information is readily available through an increasing variety of sources such as web searches, blogs, television, cell phones, video games and so on, it is important that attention is given to providing meaning over the acquisition of facts. Research points out the value of asking learners to analyse, synthesize and apply understanding in new situations. Learning has to be regarded as something that can be accomplished by all. The system must reflect this and restructure to meet the needs of every participant. A system designed to promote the top 25% of learners who will advance to post secondary school education does nothing to develop the remaining 75% who are also capable of moving forward to great things if attention is paid to developing them as learners. The school structure of the 21st century has an obligation, both morally and professionally, to create a system that allows every student to grow and develop as a learner.

What if teachers were provided the time and support to become instructional leaders for 21st century education? Teachers need to be empowered and enabled. Empowerment is giving power and authority to make decisions and enabling is to give the resources or directions to complete an assignment. Asking teachers to create a stimulating, creative, meaningful and interactive learning environment requires time, energy, training, resources and collaboration. The top down, silo based, hierarchy that dominates the educational system today, fails to provide the support required for teachers to develop the skills to become educations leaders in the 21st century. Although seldom recognized, the power for change rests almost entirely in the hands of the classroom teacher. Major decisions can be made by those in positions of authority, however, the implementation of those plans are dependent on what happens once the doors of the classroom close. Empowering teachers to become agents of change requires the recognition of them as professionals. Every opportunity must be taken to engage them in the decision making process. Teacher buy-in is critical to the future of education. Providing opportunities for teachers to work together, to share ideas, to design and develop programs and to share information is valuable for their growth as professionals. School boards have to develop and maintain an infrastructure that supports and motivates teachers to be creative in their approach and rewards them for originality and commitment.

What if society could become a reflection of what schools should be...WHAT IF?

Chapter One:
Winds of Change

Dirty fingernails, oil and grime are all part of a days work for Jim. New challenges, troubleshooting, critical thinking, suspending judgement, team work and finding practical solutions are all routine. Jim is a mechanic in a service department of an auto dealership in Chesterville, Ontario, Canada. He's been on the job for over 30 years. It all began with a short automotive service training program that helped him qualify for the job followed by an on the job apprenticeship with a qualified mechanic. Today, with so many car parts being computerized, it's almost impossible to land a job as a mechanic without going through a formal training program. Because technology is evolving at such a rapid pace, many mechanics keep current with auto technician certificate programs. Jim takes refresher courses to stay up to date with new equipment, repair techniques and diagnostics. This is the only way he can keep up with changes in fuel systems, drive trains, transmissions and braking systems.

No day is typical for Jim. He sees all kinds of cars from sedans to sports cars and hybrids to trucks. His ability to diagnose and problem solve is critical to his job. His understanding of how systems work and how each part of the system is connected to the whole allows Jim to make decisions quickly and effectively. Jim can often diagnose the problem and begin immediately with the next step required to repair the problem.

Change in the design of hybrid engine technology has put Jim back in the classroom. The faster technology changes, the more knowledge and training Jim requires. It is impossible for him to use the repair methods he was trained to use when he first began the job. Everything has changed and although he still repairs "cars", Jim's understanding and knowledge is ongoing and constantly being upgraded. He must have the desire and ability to be a life-long learner. His future depends on it.

Auto mechanics repair and maintain cars. Some mechanics work on all parts of any car, while others specialize in one area or on one type of car. The most challenging aspect of car repair is often the mechanic's favourite part: diagnosing the problem. Speed and accuracy in diagnosis and quoting prices to the customer are crucial if the mechanic intends to keep long-term clients. The mechanic examines the engine while it is running (if possible) to see if his initial assumptions are correct. Electronic diagnostic equipment is useful but the good mechanic can tell a lot by using eyes, ears, even nose, as he searches for problems and potential hazards. Sometimes he repairs parts, but if the part is worn or damaged, he replaces it.

Some mechanics compare their field to that of the physician, because most people come in only when their car is in dire straits, not when regular maintenance could have avoided the problems altogether. When people come in for an automotive check-up, mechanics often replace worn parts before they become hazardous to the driver, even though drivers can be suspicious of mechanics who recommend the replacement of parts that haven't stopped functioning.

The best mechanics have mastery of a wide variety of integrated skills: electrical systems, more complicated than an average homes; computerized electronics; fuel systems and refrigeration. Auto mechanics proudly compare themselves to doctors, since they mainly see people with complaints, whereas the human body and its problems have remained essentially unchanged for millennia, the design of cars change every year. As a result, the job requires more preparation than ever before. More and more, cars are controlled by electronic instruments, so mechanics are using computers constantly. Computers have become as much a part of the tool box as wrenches. Most auto mechanics intern while still in automotive repair school, then work full time at the same dealerships. They read trade papers daily to keep abreast of changes and trends in their industry. As they gain experience, they can move into higher-paying, specialized positions. They can also rise to the ranks of supervisor or manager, particularly if they have strong interpersonal skills to calm unsatisfied customers who are displeased by high service bills and inconvenience.

My grandfather was a mechanic his entire life. He began as a youth in the early 1930's working on motors that were archaic by today's standards. Despite the simplicity of the technology at the time, his day was no less challenging than it would have been today. Decisions were based on his understanding of the automobile systems and as they changed in design so did his need for new learning. He had to develop skills that would allow him to adapt to the world around him. Change may not have occurred as quickly as it does today but it was still a critical and vital factor for grandfather to embrace. His success as a mechanic depended on his flexibility and desire for growth.

> "Change will not come if we wait for some other person or some other time. We are the ones we've been waiting for. We are the change that we seek."
>
> —Barrack Obama

Change has become today's constant. We can all be sure that when we open our eyes in the morning, something will have changed during our hours of sleep. We cannot bury our heads in the sand and hope to ignore the winds of change that are blowing past us. By doing so, we risk having our exposed butts kicked by those who embrace the energy of change. There is precious little time to waste. Waiting for guidance and leadership to help us navigate the turbulent waters ahead only puts us at further risk. Change is around us and we are the leaders who will guide us to land.

The financial crisis of 2009 left little doubt as to the need for finding new ways of doing business. The walls of the world have come crashing down and with them come new and exciting challenges. The goblins of the global economy have been awakened. We are facing a world where only the fittest will prosper. Huge corporations have fallen and poor business practices have been exposed. Economic giants have found themselves in vulnerable positions never before experienced. Bankruptcies and foreclosure have awakened everyone to the new realities of the twenty first century. To be competitive in today's economy, everyone needs to be aware that we can no longer let the winds of change pass us by. We must turn our faces to the wind and respect its power. It can't be stopped and more important it can't be ignored.

Within minutes of the United States and Canadian governments bailing out General Motors new television commercials were being created to show that change was being embraced by the corporate giants. Promises of new commitments, awareness of needs and attention to the consumer was being publicly addressed. Mistakes of the past were being acknowledged and plans for new and better ways were being shared. Companies were openly displaying understanding of being accountable and the need to embrace change.

Domino Pizza, a dominate force in the world of "fast" food, has come forward with a series of commercials, exposing their weaknesses and their plan to address the "tastes" of the nation. They openly embrace public opinion and want their product to be evaluated and judged. They recognize that they can no longer ride the waves of past accomplishments and success. To continue to be competitive in today's economy, they must develop new skills and do things differently. The global economy not only expects "newness", it demands that it happens.

In his book, "The World Is Flat", Thomas Friedman discusses events and technologies that are "flattening" the world and increasing globalization. As this continues to happen the world will become highly interconnected without regard for distance, culture, language or individual status. He describes, in great detail, the ten significant factors that have levelled the economic playing field. The end to the "cold war" and the symbolism of the fall of the Berlin Wall was the beginning of breaking down barriers between people and ideologies. The development of the Internet in 1995 gave people access to information all over the world. The design of software standards and protocols allowed computers to better communicate with each other regardless of where they were located. These first three "flatteners", as identified by Friedman, created a collaborative platform to allow people from every part of the world to share digital information over the internet so that work and projects could be done by people regardless of where they live.

The power of the computer was enhanced by the fourth "flattener". Uploading information provided the freedom to create and contribute to the world of software development. Hierarchy in the field of program development was levelled. No longer were the creative giants the only players in the world of software development. Quality programs were being created from anywhere by anyone. Other "flatteners", outsourcing and offshoring, brought the world together. Companies were no longer restricted to doing business within their borders. Work could be done anywhere, by anyone for the best price and by the best people. Time zones were being used to allow companies to be in operation around the clock. Companies such as Wal-Mart created the next "flattener" through their creation of the Supply-Chain. Products and goods could be rapidly moved on an unimaginable scale. UPS marketed their unique skills on a global level by creating insourcing, their unique ability to get deeply involved in all aspects of a product. The development of a "hub" structure allows companies to get into areas totally unrelated to their business.

The individual's personal creative powers were strengthened by having the ability to access and develop their own supply chain of information, knowledge and entertainment. They were using the power of in-forming, thus, elevating their position in the global economy.

Finally, Friedman discusses the magnification of the first nine flatteners by the development of such things as wi-fi, instant messaging, file sharing, P2P, VoIP, video-conferencing.

The end result of the world being flattened is the increased importance of globalization. Together, people of the world are able to work to discover and solve economic, environmental, political and social problems facing each of us. The need for interdependence is upon us. With this interdependence comes the need for the skills to work in the 21st century. We are no longer living and working in isolation. The hermit has been replaced by the social butterfly. Being a valued member of the "team" is become increasingly important. There is a demand for citizens who are smarter, more creative and more capable of leading, managing, collaborating and networking with productive people around the world.

"Imagination is more important than knowledge."

—Albert Einstein

Developed nations are moving from an industrial world model to a deeper , intuitive conceptual world. Daniel Pink, author of "A Whole New Mind", points out that with this significant change, will come new ways of conducting our business practices. Pink sees three forces driving the Western world in a new and different direction: abundance: Asia; and automation. Pink suggests that each business person needs to ask three basic questions to move into the conceptual age. Answers to these questions are the essential conditions of business success for the future.

1. Can someone overseas do it cheaper?

2. Can a computer do it faster?

3. Am I offering something that satisfies the non-material, transcendent desires of an abundant age?

Abundance of materials created by left-brain thinkers has been so successful that the ultimate in planned obsolescence has finally taken over. We can now make things quicker and cheaper. Most members of developing nations have significantly more material goods than they need or will ever use. Self-storage has become a 17 billion dollar industry in the United States. More than two thirds of the population of the United States own homes and cars. Many own more than one television set. Mobile phones have become a necessity rather than a luxury. The left-brainers have been so successful that they have kept us wanting for nothing. We have become a society of affluence and when we are not storing our "rewards", we are throwing them away.

> "The United States spends more on trash bags than ninety other countries spend on everything. In other words, the receptacles of our waste cost more than all the goods consumed by nearly half of the world's nations.
>
> —Polly LaBarre

It is this prosperity, created by left-brained skills, that makes it imperative for businesses to now begin to use right brain-brain thought processes. In an age of affluence and abundance it is not enough for a company to produce a product that is functional and well priced. Companies now need to produce a product that is functional, well priced and beautiful, unique and even meaningful. A perfect example of this new product design comes in the form of designer toilet brushes and waste paper baskets. An interest has been created for things we don't really need.

Daniel Pink sees Asia as a huge contributing factor to this new age. They are a source of inexpensive labour in the area of manufacturing. Companies from highly developed nations are moving production of their products to parts of the world where it can be done cheaper. In doing so, we have left ourselves in a position where our industrial workforce is being put out of business. Technological advancement is another factor that has created a shift in economic focus. In some cases, computers have replaced the need for left-brain human traits. Any job that depends on routine steps or can be broken down into a series of repeatable steps can be replaced by a machine. Globalization has taken the business world by storm. Many jobs in the computer software and industrial technology industry will move overseas. Offshore locales such as Bangalore, India have now become the new silicon valley of the world.

The final factor Pink argues as a significant force in the new age is automation. Automation of everything from factory assembly to medical diagnosis has become common place in the new economy. Just about everything can be broken down into a series of logical steps or actions, and as a result automation, is putting us out of work because machines can do it better and faster than humans.

The time has come for what Pink calls "high-concept skills". He describes these skills as the ability to create artistically and emotionally satisfying products, to detect patterns and unexpected opportunities, to craft a satisfying story and to combine seemingly unrelated ideas into a novel invention. In addition to these specialized skills, Pink continues to argue for "high touch skills" such as being able to empathize, to understand subtleties of human interaction, to find joy in ones self, to elicit it in others and to engage in the pursuit of meaning and purpose.

> "Play will be to the 21st century what work was to the last 300 years of industrial society-our dominant way of knowing, doing and creating value."
>
> —Pat Kane

The new economy calls for skills and talents that, historically, have not been overly valued by our education system. The industrial model, dominated by left-brain logical strategists, has to make way for a new age of commerce, learning and living that will require right-brain thinkers capable of weaving their unique talents throughout the social fabric of a new society. Young people entering the workforce today can expect to change not just jobs, but occupations, several times in their working lives. There is an increased demand for freelance work, short term contracts, self-employment and entrepreneurial opportunities. International companies use workers from anywhere in the world on the basis of their skills. Young people need a high level of skills for this complex new world. They also need to be able to adapt to change and to new opportunities.

> "You're not going to find the meaning of life hidden under a rock written by someone else. You'll only find it by giving meaning to life from inside yourself."
>
> —Dr. Robert Firestone

Businesses everywhere have to compete in a world that is changing faster than ever. To keep pace, they need people who can consistently generate new ideas and adapt to constant change. Growing demand in businesses world-wide is for forms of education and training that develops human resources and in particular the powers of communication, innovation and creativity. Where companies of yesterday used to be concerned with industry and manufacturing, corporations today are moving into the fields of communication, information, entertainment, science and technology. With the levelling of the economic playing field, businesses need "learners" who can successfully balance knowledge and skills while developing innovative and creative ideas. In addition, there is a need to understand and respect different cultural values and traditions and the processes of cultural development. Businesses everywhere are saying it is becoming very difficult to find these people. One of the significant reasons for this has to do with our educational system. All over the world, formal educational systems wrestle with strategies to raise their standards of education. Literacy and numeracy skills continue to take on extreme importance. Testing of these skills has become a dominant force in setting the direction of future learning. Creativity and cultural awareness does not easily fit into an educational system that is based on the industrial age model and a narrow view of intelligence.

The foundations of the present education system were laid at the end of the nineteenth century. Schools were designed to meet the needs of a world that was being changed by industrialization and a workforce that was roughly 80% manual labour and 20% professional. The system prioritized and structured subjects that appeared relevant to working life, including math, language and science. An emphasis was placed on academic ability based on success in these subject areas. Students were sorted according to their "abilities". The system was very successful for that time and met the needs of society. Those with a basic education found manual jobs and those few who went on with post secondary education were rewarded with a passport for a successful career as a professional.

"Many of our schools are good schools if only this were 1965."

—Louise Stoll and Dean Fink

The present day educational system, still modelled on the old system, is not designed to create the learner required for the 21st century. Out of the Industrial Revolution came the need for conformity and the educational system has followed its lead and delivered in spades. We mass produce our students as if they were products on an assembly line. It is a system based on silos. Students are scanned and processed by age, by intellect, by subjects and by future plans. Curriculum content and the resulting "test" are the drivers of the system and few teachers dare to move beyond the confines of the "bus" out of fear of not "preparing" their students for the next stage on the academic conveyor belt.

> "If we are to prepare successfully for the twenty-first century, we will have to do more than just improve literacy and numeracy skills. We need a broad, flexible and motivating education that recognises the different talents of all children and delivers excellence for everyone."
>
> —White Paper Excellence in School, British Government 1997

Ken Robinson, international speaker and author, explains that there are two factors that have created a need for a change in the educational system: the emergence of the knowledge economy and the demand for intellectual labour and population growth. The academic currency of the past has changed. No longer is a college or university degree a ticket for success. Over the next few years an increasing number of people will gain academic qualifications. The percentage of highly educated people will be greater than ever before. A degree or certificate will no longer be a guarantee of employment. The minimum requirement for entry into the field of professional work is on the rise due partly to the sheer number of available workers. Companies should be smiling when they see the level of the competition for job placements, however, despite the number of graduates available, businesses are reporting that too many graduates cannot meet the "new" demands of the economic world. They are finding it very difficult to hire graduates who can communicate, work in teams, problem solve, are adaptable, empathetic or think creatively. Academic qualifications alone are not enough. Employers are looking for qualities and aptitudes which academic qualifications are not designed to produce. Key corporations today are deeply involved in the fields of communications, information, entertainment, science and technology. The success of these companies depend on finding workers who can invent, associate, connect reflect, generate and put into action new ideas.

"According to former Secretary of Education, Richard Riley, the top ten in demand jobs in 2010 did not exist in 2004. We are currently preparing students for jobs that don't yet exist, using technologies that haven't been invented in order to solve problems we don't even know are problems yet."

—Karl Fisch Shift Happens 4.0

We can no longer live in the past and maintain systems and models that were based on the needs of yesterday. Students entering school in 2010 may be retiring around the year 2055. During the span of their working life, they will most likely change occupations several times. Many will be working at jobs that don't presently exist, in businesses that don't exist, using skills that are yet to be determined with equipment that has not yet been imagined. The changes facing the world today are not just economic but also cultural. How we live, how we relate to each other, what we believe, what we think about and value, are the cornerstones of the new revolution. The educational system is expected to give people the skills and qualities they need to be successful and productive citizens. The government's response to this demand is to increase the standards of learning and although there is nothing wrong with improving the quality of education, one has to ask if the standards we are raising are the standards that meet the needs of a new generation. There can be no successful argument against students having a sound understanding of literacy, mathematics and science. These will always be critical components of a students' learning, however, the time is here for us to address "new" skills for the learners in the 21st century. The world has changed and so, too, must we as educators. Today's learners need to become lifelong learners. They need to be taught how to learn and relearn, how to be effective and contributing members of a team, how to work with different cultures and how to be creative in their thinking.

> "For a student starting a four year technical or college degree this means that half of what they learn in the first year will be outdated by their third year of study.
>
> —Karl Fisch Shift Happens 4.0

It has been known for some time what students will need and be able to do in the 21st Century. The SCANS report, "What Work Requires of Schools", in 1991, clearly outlined 21st Century Learning as learning built on the foundation of basic knowledge but went well beyond the basics to include a significant set of "new" skills. This report showed a profound understanding of the coming changes of the millennium including globalization and the increased role of technology in work and life. It was one of the first reports to document the need for students to be better communicators, collaborators, and creators for the workplace and society. The report goes further to emphasize the need for the development of thinking skills, personal qualities such as responsibility and self-management, project management, interpersonal skills in teams, information skills, system skills and technology utilization skills.

In "Learning for the 21st Century", issued in 2003, the Partnership for 21st Century Skills continued to update the skills required for the learner in the 21ˢᵗ Century. Again, learning builds on the core subjects, but shows that 21ˢᵗ Century learning includes information and communication skills, thinking skills and problem solving skills, interpersonal and self-direction skills and skills to utilize 21ˢᵗ Century tools such as information and communication technologies. What was pointed out in this report is the importance of assessment and feedback to students as they move towards mastery of the 21ˢᵗ century skills.

Tony Wagner, co-director of the Change Leadership Group at Harvard University's Graduate School of Education, presents a list of seven "survival skills" that students will need to succeed in today's information-age. In his book "The Global Achievement Gap: Why Even Our Best Schools Don't Teach the New Survival Skills our Children Need–And What We Can Do About It", Wagner claims it is a school's job to make sure students have these skills before leaving. These skills are:

1. Problem-solving and critical thinking

2. Collaboration across networks and leading by influence

3. Agility and adaptability

4. Initiative and entrepreneurship

5. Effective written and oral communication

6. Accessing and analysing information: and

7. Curiosity and imagination

Some nations around the world are paying attention to the needs of the new world order. In Canada, United States and parts of Europe and Asia, leaders are attempting to address the need for change in the educational system. The slogan in Singapore is "Thinking Schools, Learning Nation". The educational leaders in Singapore are making changes to the way they educate their youth. They want to develop a willingness to learn in all their students. They want them to experiment, be innovative and to take risks.

The United Kingdom has committed billions of dollars to rebuild their educational system over a 10 to 15 year period. The Building Schools for the Future program mission is "Working together to create world-class, 21st century schools – environments which will inspire learning for decades to come and provide exceptional assets to the whole community".

It has become very clear what students need to learn and be able to do for the 21st century. The key questions now are: How do they learn these skills? How will student know they have the skills? What will a 21st Century school and program look like? In other words, how will we provide the students the opportunities to develop these skills and how will we know when they have them?

There is no doubt that the list of skills is extensive. The question that remains is how can all of these skills be built into the curriculum, and at the same time, develop competencies in the core subjects? A traditional approach to teaching, where students typically work alone, work on unrelated, short non-complex assignments that emphasize short-term content memorization, write for the teacher alone and rarely make presentations, cannot be used for the development of these skills. It can be done if students are given the opportunity to work on projects that are designed to elicit collaboration, critical thinking, written communication, while simultaneously meeting the content standards.

"Only in education, never in the life of the farmer, sailor, merchant, physician, or laboratory experimenter, does knowledge mean primarily a store of information aloof from doing."

—John Dewey

Project based or problem based learning takes a completely different approach. Project-based learning is often confused with projects, which are short activities injected into traditional education to create a brief moment of excitement, usually at the conclusion of a unit. Real Project-Based Learning is deep, complex and rigorous. Students work in teams or partnerships on an in-depth assignment for a specific amount of time. Basic team skills are introduced and practised during the project. The theme of the assignment should be based around the creation of a complex essential question that will be answered at the completion of the project. The activities are scaffolded and new information is presented that helps develop a deeper understanding of the topic. Skills such as oral communication, written communication, teamwork, critical thinking and problem solving are formally presented to the students and are reinforced throughout the project.

Feedback and assessment are ongoing and critical to the development of these skills. A student can't get better or become a manager of his own learning without constant, real-time assessment and feedback. This is called assessment for learning rather than of learning. Assessment for learning starts with outcomes, proceeds with projects, products and performances that connect to the outcomes and completes the loop with feedback for the student.

The project should finish with a formal presentation that shows understanding of the content and answers to the essential question. Students need to conclude their experience with self-reflection or meta-cognition. It is important for the students to see themselves as learners and know what the next step is for improvement.

As our students move forward into the 21st century, they will need to be prepared to meet the challenges of the new global community. Students will need to move beyond basic competencies in core subject areas. To be effective members of the world of work and to contribute as productive members of their communities, students will be required to develop skills that will allow them to actively compete in a highly competitive world market that has expanded beyond boundaries. Critical thinking and problem solving skills will be important for all students as they approach new challenges and opportunities. Effective collaboration and communication skills will be required as the students engage in a world of local and global networking, selling ideas, creating designs, displaying empathy, carefully crafting stories. New technologies and work strategies will require agility and adaptability as students find themselves in turbulent and often uncharted water. Being capable of accessing, analysing and seeing the significance of information and data will be increasingly important as the information explosion expands.

The same skills that will give the students a competitive advantage, in the world of work, will also provide them with the requirements to be good citizens. The people of the world must face many difficult challenges and serious problems must be solved. With new technological advancements comes a myriad of serious environmental, ethical and moral questions that must be addressed. Today's learners must be prepared to meet the many challenges of the 21st century. They must be given the opportunity to develop these skills.

Chapter Two:
The Learner in the 21st Century

"Much of what passes for educational best practices these days are merely vestiges of a bygone era. For better or for worse, the electronic age has radically reshaped human thought and behaviour. Clinging to educational practices designed to teach "data classification" helps no one – especially the students who are facing a world radically different than the one our schools prepare them for."

—Kyle Mathews, Dream With In

By the end of the 20th century, the public education system was lacking in many ways. The problem was a disconnect between the knowledge taught in schools, and the knowledge needed to survive and grow in life. Schools did not keep up with the changing industrialized society or with the sciences. Educators taught with rigidity: straight rows of desks, teachers lecturing, memorization of facts and figures, knowledge cut off from the everyday lives and experiences of students. There was no student-centred learning, no learning by doing, no enthusiasm for lifelong learning.

The purpose of education should be to gain knowledge useful for real life and for building moral character and growth of the whole person: intellectually, personally, socially, and profession-ally. Education must represent life, and it must be available to every member of society. Despite our increased understanding of how students learn and the implementations of new teaching strategies, one must ask, "Has our system changed significantly over the past one hundred years and are we meeting the needs of society?"

> "My parents told me, 'Finish your dinner. People in China and India are starving.' I tell my daughters, "Finish your homework, people in India and China are starving for your job."
>
> —Thomas L. Friedman

Globalization is flattening the world and challenging nations as never before, as pointed out by Thomas Friedman in his book, The World is Flat, students in North America and other advanced nations around the world must meet the challenge and lead a new era of global cooperation as 21st century learners. Society needs citizens who are smarter, more creative and capable of leading, managing, collaborating and networking with productive people around the globe. Educators need to be totally aware of their responsibility for providing a climate that will develop and enhance 21st century skills. The educational standards need to be upgraded to world-class standards. Opportunities must be provided for students to become problem solvers, team workers, critical thinkers and effective communicators.

> "There's a dark little joke exchanged by educators with a dissident streak: Rip Van Winkle awakens in the 21st century after a hundred-year snooze and is, of course, utterly bewildered by what he sees. Men and women dash about, talking to small metal devices pinned to their ears. Young people sit at home on sofas, moving miniature athletes around on electronic screens. Older folk defy death and disability with metronomes in their chests and with hips made of metal and plastic. Airports,

hospitals, shopping malls – every place Rip goes just baffles him. But when he finally walks into a school-room, the old man knows exactly where he is. 'This is a school,' he declares. 'We used to have these back in 1906. Only now the blackboards are green.'"

—How to Bring Our Schools Out of the 20th Century, Claudia Willis, Time CNN Article 2006

There is a need to rethink, redesign and reconstruct our school system to enable a "students at work" environment for the development of 21st century skills. Our schools must be structured to reflect our understanding of how people learn. The cookie cutter approach to school design will not meet the needs of the new learner. Creating a successful learning environment that will foster team work, collaboration, critical thinking and problem solving requires changes in the physical environment, a new understanding of scheduling and time management, the development of a technical infrastructure, and opportunities to connect with various learning communities.

The main factor for the design of a 21st century structure is based on flexibility. The physical structure of our schools today, based on the industrial era, cannot attempt to meet the multifaceted demands facing us globally. Change is happening at such a rapid pace that no one can predict where technology and new teaching strategies will take us. Because of this, our buildings must be designed as moveable, flexible structures, easily transforming into the needs of the moment. Furniture must be easily moved with adjustable walls. The creation of learning spaces need to be formed that will provide opportunities for social interaction, to inspire creativity and to foster intellectual engagement.

Being flexible with the design of our schools is only one step in the creation of a 21st century learning environment. Flexibility must also be reflected in the way our schools manage time. The industrial model of education built around a 19th century calendar of ten months, scheduled holidays, specific length of the instructional day and "seated time" for subject credit is unacceptable for the development of the skills of the 21st century. Project based learning and cross-curricular studies requires blocks of study time. Scheduling time during the school day for students and staff to collaborate and plan is an important step to creating a fertile learning environment. The need for teachers to share and discuss with colleagues strategies for presenting and assessing the "new" skills being taught requires time to be built into their schedules.

It must be recognized that not all quality learning takes place within the walls of the school or during regular school hours. Learning does not always happen on the clock. Unlike a title fight between two heavy weight boxers, learning does not begin and end with the bell. Schools need to pay attention to the many ways students learn that go beyond tradition. Co-op placements, internships, online learning and community service can each develop deep and rich learning experiences. Alternative approaches to learning beyond the walls of the classroom, should be encouraged and recognized. What is most important is that students master the concepts and skills. It should not matter how and where learning occurs nor the time spent to accomplish it. Attention must be given to both the formal and informal learning of each student. With the recognition of flexibility in time management comes the need for new assessment strategies that will guide subject mastery and application. The traditional methods of evaluating student performance will not be sufficient.

The design of an effective technological infrastructure is required to support learning. Students need access to tools and resources that will allow them to explore, become aware of and show their understanding. Teachers and administrators also need tools to research, interact and share. Technology is required to assist educators with the data required to effectively do their jobs. The most important goal of technology is to assist and support people as they acquire knowledge and share understanding. Technology by itself will not develop the skills for the 21st century learner. Like any tool, its effectiveness is based on the user's competency in applying it. Technology needs to be integrated into curriculum delivery. To accomplish this, a system must be employed to support both the teachers and the students.

Never has the saying, "It takes a village to raise a child", been so true. Changes in the physical structure of our buildings, the management of time and the integration of technology can only become effective when we create a community partnership with all of those involved in education. A positive, interactive culture needs to be created that supports a climate of respect and trust among the students and adults. Positive and productive relationships need to be established that will allow the mission to be carried out. All partners need to be on the same page, learning for everyone, children and adults alike. Teachers and schools can no longer be silos of isolation. Everyone has to be aware that there is a world beyond the walls of their school. A commitment on the part of everyone is required. Schools will need to develop a plan based on their school culture, teaching talents, resources, instructional strategies and the effectiveness of their leadership, while keeping their sights on the mission plan shared by all.

> "...to make each one of our schools an embryonic community life, active with the types of occupations that reflect the life of the larger community, and permeated throughout with the spirit of art, history, and science. When the school introduces and trains each child of society into membership within such a little community, saturating him with spirit of service, and providing him with the instruments of effective self-direction, we shall have the deepest and best guarantee of a larger society which is worthy, lovely and harmonious."
>
> —John Dewey

The 21st century requires a new way of educating our children, one that breaks through the silos that have separated schools from the real world and educators from each other. Political leaders have to become aware of the needs of the 21st century and make a commitment to creating and supporting a system that will develop these skills. Our students need a learning environment that allows collaboration and sharing of information and ideas across boundaries, an environment that promotes cultural diversity, and fosters a culture of mutual respect. The schools of tomorrow need to be flexible in their arrangement of space, time, technology and people. All learners need to be able to unite around the world to discuss global challenges and opportunities. The question is, "Who will bring about this change?"

The Power of One

Change is the key to the success of our students and to their future. Often, however, change is something we fiercely resist. The system can only become what it needs to be through a significant change in the way we provide learning opportunities for our students. In spite of knowing what needs to be done, educators find it difficult to move beyond their comfort zone. Even when new strategies and achievement opportunities are presented and encouraged, many educators are still too comfortable in their old ways to make an adjustment. The irony is that if change is going to take place, it must begin with the teacher's mind set. A paradigm shift in thinking and the way we see ourselves as educators is the first step towards becoming effective teachers in the 21st century. Change begins in the minds of our teachers and the future of education rests in the desire and ability to master this change. Too often, people wait for change to be directed from those working in positions of authority. Waiting for this dynamic shift in educational thinking is not something that is going to happen quickly. Historically, changes in education have been slow, due in part to the political "machine" that directs education. The demand for educational reform is not new. It has been discussed in great detail for the past one hundred years beginning with great philosophers such as John Dewey. The very first place to look for change and transformation is with each of us.

The biggest obstacles to change are fear, lack of motivation, lack of knowledge and lack of vision. People will not change if they fear failure, if they don't have a reason to, if they don't know how to or if they don't know where change will take them. Many require evidence that the proposed changes will be an improvement. To inspire change in others, you have to make their future rewards stronger than their current fears. If changes are to be lasting and successful, it is essential to have the necessary reinforcement and tools to assist in the transformation process. Educators must have desire, coupled with enthusiasm and passion. They must be open to suggestions, input and new ideas. Nothing is going to change if they keep doing the same things they've been doing all along. They must be open to new possibilities, new ways of thinking and new ways of doing things. People can't act differently if they don't think differently, and they can't think differently if they aren't open to new information.

Providing learning opportunities beyond the traditional teaching strategies is the first step to providing a 21st century learning environment. There is extensive and well documented evidence about the kinds of teaching approaches that consistently have a positive impact on student learning. This research tells us that students learn best when teachers create a supportive learning environment, encourage reflective thinking and action, make new learning relevant, encourage shared learning and make connections to prior learning and experience.

"I never teach my pupils; I only attempt to provide the conditions in which they can learn."

—Albert Einstein

Students grow when they feel accepted and when a positive relationship is established with other students and teachers. Students need an environment that is caring, inclusive, non-discriminatory and cohesive. A bond of trust needs to be formed. The establishment of trust with students is critical to creating a positive learning environment. Learners need to know that they can trust teachers, and more importantly, that they too are seen as trustworthy. One way of creating this trust is to give students ownership of their learning. The more students feel they have a choice and a voice in their learning, the more the students will become engaged in the learning process. Providing students with the opportunity to lead a team or discussion groups allows them the freedom to freely express their ideas. The use of weekly student-lead classroom meetings and monthly divisional meetings creates an environment where the students are accepting responsibility for what is happening around them. Giving the student the opportunity to set the agenda, to establish the meeting norms and to freely discuss concerns shows the students that teachers care about what is important to them.

Learning becomes effective when students develop the ability to be objective by suspending judgement before they make a decision or come to a conclusion. Reflective learners assimilate new learning by making connections with what they already know, adapting it to their own purpose and putting the thought into action. With experience and opportunity, the students will develop their creativity, their ability to think critically about ideas and information and develop the ability to reflect on their own thinking (metacognition). These skills are enhanced when teachers design tasks that require students to critically evaluate the resources they use and consider the purpose for which the material was originally created.

Learning is most engaging when students understand what they are learning, why they are learning it and how they will be able to use it. Effective teaching experiences should stimulate the curiosity of the students, requiring them to search for relevant information and ideas and challenging them to use or apply what they have discovered in new contexts or in new ways. In doing this, students are seeing the relevance of what they are learning and become more engaged in their learning. Every attempt should be made to answer the "why" and "how" questions up front. Engagement and relevancy are deeply connected throughout the learning process.

> "People don't care what you know until they know that you care."
>
> —Anonymous

Students need to share their excitement for learning with others, including classmates, family members and people in the wider community. They need an audience to show their under-standing and to reinforce their learning. Teachers can encourage this process by having the class work as a learning community. Students need to feel that they are part of a learning environment where everyone is a learner, including the teacher. Shared learning experiences must be encouraged with ongoing support and readily available feedback.

> "For learning to take place with any kind of efficiency, students must be motivated. To be motivated, they must become interested. And they become interested when they are actively working on projects which they can relate to their values and goals in life."
>
> —Gus Tuberville, President, William Penn College

Students learn best when they are able to integrate new learning with what they already know and understand. Building on what the students know and have experienced maximizes the use of learning time and anticipates students' learning needs.

Making connections across learning areas and to the wider community is valuable for creating engagement in the learner.

> "The integrated curriculum is a great gift to experienced teachers. It's like getting a new pair of lenses that make teaching a lot more exciting and help us look forward into the next century. It is helping students take control of their own learning."

> —M. Markus, media specialist, quoted in Shoemaker, September 1991

Students that enter our schools in the 21st century do not resemble the students being taught forty or fifty years ago. The existing educational model that many schools operate under today, produce the learners that were required during a time of high industrialization. An understanding of compliance, order and routine, were requirements that helped people flourish during that era. Technology was in its infant stage and had little or no impact on the learning environment. Similarly, technology had no impact on the daily lives of our students.

> "Kids should be seen and not heard."

> —My Father and many others (1950's)

Throughout the 20th century model of education, success in school was defined by an individual's competency in two subject areas; literacy and mathematics. Those who did well in these subject areas were set on a pathway that led to post secondary school education. Those who struggled in these areas were ushered out the door into the world of work or manual labour. Creative thinking, problem solving and collaboration were not skills viewed as necessary and never addressed. There was no strong need for theses skills in the workforce or in society in general. Innovation and creative thought were left in the hands of a few who possessed these skills in some inherent way.

All young people have different abilities, capacities and aptitudes. They have different environmental influences and social conditions under which they were raised. They each have a uniquely different past and a different future. One of the roles of education should be to help students find their future and understand their past. This begins by helping students discover their own passions, special interests, strengths and sensibilities. There is no question of the need for students to possess strong literacy skills, however, their needs go beyond academics. Social, emotional and spiritual interests must be as considered as well. Young people today want their educational experiences to be meaningful. They have a need to discover who they are and how they fit into the world around them. Schools must find ways to help students explore and express their own emotions and feelings in positive and constructive ways.

Ability comes in many different forms and should not be defined only by traditional criteria. A student's academic abilities will not necessarily guarantee success in the 21st century. Every student has capabilities and strengths beyond academics. Children with high academic abilities may also have strengths beyond academics. Students who struggle with literacy and mathematics may have other strengths that have been neglected or gone unnoticed. The key is to find what our students are good and at to give them the opportunities to develop in these areas. Self confidence and self esteem will rise and, often, so will overall academic performance.

The problems of the world require people who understand what it means to be human in the 21st century. Life is so much more than the world of work. Learners need to know that the high-level skills they learn in school today are also needed for them to be effective and contributing citizens of tomorrow.

"Today's child is bewildered when he enters the 19th century environment that still characterizes the educational establishment, where information is scarce but ordered and structured by fragmented, classified patterns, subjects, and schedules."

—Marshall McLuhan, 1967

Today's learners are unique. Students growing up in the twenty first century have the world at their fingertips. Young people today are totally connected and engaged in the world around them. On any day, a young person is faced with a universe full of media which includes 200 plus cable television networks, 5,500 consumer magazine titles, 10,500 radio stations, 30 million websites, and 122,000 newly published books. To the average adult, this is a world beyond our grasp. Today's students are literally born to a world of media choice that places them firmly in control of their media environment.

While teens and young adults are exposed to many different types of media, a study conducted by a leading global Internet company, Carat North America, reveals that the internet surpasses them all in the amount of time spent, which in an average week is as follows:

(1) 16.7 hours online (excluding email),

(2) 13.6 hours watching TV,

(3) 12 hours listening to the radio,

(4) 7.7 hours talking on the phone,

(5) Six hours reading books and magazines (personal, not scholastic).

The study, which polled more than 2,500 teens and young adults, between the ages of 13-24, revealed that the ability to personalize and manage the media experience and content, was the primary reason this group chooses the Internet over other forms of media. Survey findings also showed that teens use the Internet as a primary media source while other forms of media are used as a starting point. While other generations were more likely to be connected to a single type of media, the study showed that today's teens and young adults are not overwhelmed by the abundance of media choices like cable stations, networks, magazines and radio, but rather feel empowered by it and are able to multi-task, using more than one form of media at a time, more than any other generation.

Students today expect to be engaged in everything they do. Past generations did not have this burning desire to be connected to their learning experiences. There were no video games, no MP3s, none of today's technological wonders. Our lives were less consumed by media, communication and creative opportunities. The difference between today's learner and yesterday's is that most of them already have something in their lives that is totally engaging. They have things that they do and that they are good at, something that is engaging and has a creative aspect to it. The opportunities for youth to explore their creativity are endless. Some download songs, play video games, write and mix songs, make movies or create personal websites. They all have something to keep them occupied. Some students in primary grades have multiple email addresses. Many junior students have mastered the skill of text messaging. Today's students with a computer at home can sit in their bedrooms with a number of windows open, while playing a video game and chatting on their cell phone at the same time. It can be argued that with so much going on at one time, multitasking prevents in depth learning. Regardless of the effects of multitasking, this is the environment our students live in. The world today is much different from the one many of us grew up in, however, as busy as life has become, one can never say that today's youth are unengaged.

The learner in the 21st century is a multi-tasker who uses sound and images to convey content whenever possible. Text, which was the primary medium for older generations, is tolerated only when technology is not available. Today's generation of communicators prefers to use acronyms to express their thoughts rather than well formed sentences. Those of us not well connected to the world of chat lines find it difficult to understand the significance of "LOL" or "CUL8R". That is not to say that we should place less importance on traditional forms of communication, it just makes us aware of the realities of our learners and the way they prefer to communicate.

Many of the students today spend enormous amounts of money and time on video games. The infatuation for these activities indicates the pervasive role entertainment plays in the culture of the 21st century. There is much debate concerning the value and effects these activities have on the learner. What is important to note is the insight it provides for us on student engagement.

> "I could have nothing to do, and I'll find something on the internet."
>
> —Student comment, Born To Be Wild Conference 2003

There is no question about the importance of technology in the lives of our students. Instead of debating the value of technology in education, we should be looking at the many ways we can use technology as a way to empower today's students. If a device can do something faster, more efficiently, more accurately and connects to the realities of our learners, why not use it? We need to focus less on the technology itself and more on the capabilities of these tools to empower and engage the learner. We need to provide the opportunities for students to use technology for learning. They need to learn how to use technology to their advantage.

The students growing up in the 21st century have characteristics that are often unfamiliar to older generations. These learners tend to gravitate toward group activities. Many are engaged in extracurricular activities in and out of school. They are fascinated with new technology and are comfortable with ethnic diversity. Most are digitally literate and extremely social. They crave interactivity and are good at reading visual images. Many have strong visual-spatial skills and tend to access information through a parallel process and prefer inquiry-based learning. They tend to look for fast responses and quick answers. Today's students find it difficult to learn in isolation. They prefer to work in teams with peer interaction in an environment that is structured and flexible. They become engaged in learning when they are provided with the opportunity to explore learning first hand. They would rather reach their own conclusions and find their own results than have the answers provided for them.

> "Our students have changed radically. Today's students are no longer the people our educational system was designed to teach."
>
> —Marc Prensky Digital Immigrants, Digital Natives

The simple fact is the depth of information in the world today is growing almost as quickly as new technology develops. Data is only the touch of a button away. Because of this information growth and instant availability, schools must place less importance on the memorization of material and more on evaluating the validity of information, making connections, thinking through issues and solving problems. Schools cannot teach students everything they need to know to become successful beyond school. Students no longer need to absorb vast amounts of information. Learning how to learn has become significantly more important. Students and teachers, must become life-long learners.

Tony Warner author and co-director of the Change Leadership Group at Harvard University's Graduate School of Education, discusses the importance of creating a "challenging and rigorous" educational experience for our students. He expresses his concern for the present day delivery of education to the 21st learner by introducing the idea of the "three R's" of rigor, relevance and respectful relationships. Working with a group of principals in Kona, Hawaii, a basic rubric was created to assess the level of rigor in classrooms. Rigor, as defined by Wagner and the group, relates directly to what society demands from our students when they graduate, the skills needed for work, citizenship and life-long learning. Their definition has less to do with how demanding the material covered is and more with what competencies students have actually mastered. Seven questions were created that would be used during the groups observations of classes they visited to assess the level of rigor in advanced placement courses. Students were selected at random and asked the following questions:

1. What is the purpose of this lesson?

2. Why is this important to learn?

3. In what way am I challenged to think in this lesson?

4. How will I apply, assess, or communicate what I have learned?

5. How will I know how good my work is and how I can improve it?

6. Do I feel respected by other students in this class?

7. Do I feel respected by the teacher in this class?

Upon completion of their "learning walks", the following observations were made:

> "...the primary competency students were being asked to master was the ability to memorize copious amounts of information for the test. Teachers' questions to students tended to be almost entirely related to factual

recall. In our opinion, not a single one of the AP (Advanced Placement) classes we saw was sufficiently rigorous to prepare students for work, citizenship and continuous learning in today's world."

—Tony Wagner, Rigor on Trial, 2006 The Home of Education and Teacher Magazine

Our schools are not very good at engaging the 21st century learner. Too much time and energy is being expended on test scores and rote learning without relevance. The traditional approach to engagement and motivation, using a reward system of marks are not as effective as we think, in fact they are probably counter-productive to learning in the 21st century. Daniel Pink argues in his book "Drive" that the extrinsic motivation, such as the carrot and stick approach, often does not work because they narrow the focus. These simple rewards work very well if the tasks are mundane, have clear guidelines and can't be outsourced or automated, however, where creativity is needed, much more is required to motivate the learner. Extrinsic rewards, such as grades and privileges, are not enough to ensure engagement and motivation. Pink suggests the need for deeper intrinsic rewards. Pink defines intrinsic rewards in terms of autonomy, mastery and purpose. Autonomy is the desire we have to direct our own lives, how we feel about learning and work. Mastery is our urge to get better and better at something that matters. We keep on working at something if we feel we are making steady progress. Purpose is the desire to do what we do in the service of something larger than ourselves. People will do almost anything if they feel they are making a difference and if they think it really matters. Motivation increases when we make the learning experience real, relevant, enduring and with opportunity for action. The motivation for engagement comes from within and, as a result, true learning takes place. Real learning is achieved when the joy of learning is its own reward.

"If there is anything fundamental about our nature it's the capacity for interest. Some things facilitate it. Some things undermine it."

—Daniel Pink, Drive

Schools can produce confidante, enthusiastic, responsible and motivated learners when students are given praise for the process they engage in rather than being told how smart, talented or gifted they are. School needs to encourage a mindset that fosters growth and on-going development and rewards students for effort, practice and hard work. All students need to see themselves as learners and each of them must believe that they have great potential for growth and achievement. Effort is the critical factor and must be reinforced to maintain motivation and engagement.

"For much of my life I have lived with a fixed mind set. During my middle and high school years, I convinced myself that I was not as smart as others or, on my really pretentious days, smarter than others. This thinking was a direct product of my environment. Every day, there was chatter surrounding class rankings, SAT scores, intelligence quotient, grades, and so on. I don't think it was until college, or maybe until I started teaching that I truly valued learning as an opportunity for growth. I think that most teachers want their students to relish in learning, but some students may not know how. Teaching students about growth mind sets seems invaluable."

—Lisa Rei Standford New's, Standford Report, Service February 2007

Stanford University Psychology professor Carol Dweck co-author of "Implicit Theories of Intelligence Predict Achievement Across Adolescent Transition: A Longitudinal Study and an Intervention." and the book Mindset: The New Psychology of Success, discusses the importance of developing positive mind sets in our students. She concludes through her research studies that student motivation is directly connected to how schools defined them as learners and how the students internalize their successes and failures. Many see themselves as born either smart or not. School testing confirms the learner's self-theory. According to Dweck, people's self-theories about intelligence have a profound influence on their motivation to learn. Students who hold a "fixed" theory are mainly concerned with how smart they are. Successful students prefer tasks they can already do well and avoid new learning involving risk because of the chance of failure. They spend a great deal of time and energy looking for the right answer and avoid asking questions that may give evidence of a lack of understanding. Struggling students see themselves as incapable of learning and simple don't try. These students, who encounter difficulties and poor results, are led to believe that they lack ability, and this lack of ability leads them to attribute their problems to a defect in themselves, something they have no control over. So they retire from learning, avoid investing effort in learning which would only lead to disappointment and struggle to find other ways to build up their self-esteem.

In contrast, Dweck states, students who believe in an "expandable" or "growth" theory of intelligence, want to challenge themselves to increase their abilities, even if they fail at first. These students see learning as a result of their continual effort and find learning easier and take setbacks in their stride. What students think shapes how they are motivated and what they can learn. Although most children probably fall on the continuum between these two theories, motivational factors affect their persistence, learning goals, and the desire to strive for success. As put forth by Daniel Pink, we ought to keep these ideas in mind about teaching and learning and focus on creating motivating environments for both teachers and students to achieve autonomy, personal mastery and a sense of purpose.

"What was important was the motivation. The students were energized by the idea that they could have an impact on their mind." Dweck recalled a young boy who was a ringleader of the troublemakers. "When we started teaching this idea about the mind being malleable, he looked up with tears in his eyes, and he said, 'You mean, I don't have to be dumb?'" she said. "A fire was lit under him."

—Lisa Trei, Standford New's, Standford Report, Service February 2007

All students want to know that we believe in them and that, with hard work, they can improve. Our students want to be challenged, they want to be engaged them in their learning experiences. They need us to connect to their passions, to meet them at their own level, to allow them to "interact" with their learning experiences and to be empowered by choosing how they will demonstrate their learning. Students live in a world of digital, audio and text. Every part of a student's life is filled with multimedia experiences. Because of this, students expect a similar approach in the classroom. Teacher lectures, reading assignments and chapter questions will not keep a student's interest in the 21st century. Today's students want to make a difference, they just need their educators to give them the chance.

"...before we can start doing things the right way, we've got to recognize that we've been doing them the wrong way – which most pedagogies and administrators and even most parents still refuse to accept. Today's child is growing up absurd because he is suspended between two worlds and two value systems, neither of which inclines him to maturity because he belongs wholly to neither but exists in a hybrid limbo of constantly conflicting values. The challenge of the new era is simply the total creative process of growing up – and mere teaching and repetition of facts are as irrelevant to this process as a dowser to a nuclear power plant. To expect a "turned on" child of the electric age to respond to the old education modes is rather like expecting an eagle to swim. It's simply not within his environment, and therefore incomprehensible."

—Marshall McLuhan, Playboy Interview, 1994

Comedian Bill Cosby once sang a metaphorical song called "Little Ole Man". It was about a person who sat on the railroad tracks each day, only to be hit by a train. He knew that the train was coming, but he could not apply that knowledge to get out of the way. That circumstance sounds hauntingly familiar to what is happening in education today. Everyone knows what is happening around us, we can see what is coming down the tracks, we understand the "new" learners, we have read the research on brain development, we openly acknowledge the failures of the present system. All of the state-of-the -art knowledge leaves us with one nagging question: "Why can't anything get done?" Everyone is talking about the problems and many creative solutions have been discussed yet nothing seems to change. Ideas and knowledge are very powerful but they don't become useful until they can be put into action. Knowledge is not power unless it can be implemented.

A little ole' man was sittin' on a step

And a tear trickled down his cheek.

I said "What's the matter?"

He said "A train just ran over me."

I said "Hmm. How often does this happen?

"He said "Everyday about this time."

I said "Well, why do you just sit out here then?"

He said "Cause I cannot believe that this happened."
I said "Reach out, take my hand, you'll understand."

—Bill Cosby "Little Ole Man"

Many educators, politicians and parents find it very difficult to relate to this new paradigm of education in the 21st century. It is not easy for them to make personal connections to what they don't understand. This is a huge change in our society and in the way we view education. James A. Belasco in his book "Teaching the Elephant to Dance," uses an excellent analogy for what is happening today. Belasco talks about creating change in organizations, such as business and industry, in order to cope with the changing world of the 1990's. Belasco explains that young circus elephants are trained not to move by being shackled with heavy chains to stakes deeply embedded in the ground. When the elephant is fully grown, it remembers its early training and won't try to break away even though it has only a small metal bracelet around its feet, untethered at that. Educational institutions, like many other organizations, get set in their ways as they get older. Many are held back by self-imposed bonds they have the power to break, but don't. "We've always done it this way" is the rationale for their inertia. However, if the circus tent catches fire, and the elephant smells the smoke and sees the flames, the conditioned response is overcome and the elephant moves. Belasco recommends that we find a way to get people to smell the smoke and see the flames – without actually burning down the tent. Teaching this elephant to dance is going to be a major challenge, and it will have to encompass everything from teacher and administrative professional development to educating everyone else beyond the walls of the schools. This paradigm shift requires education for a changed attitude and mind set. It is time for the elephant to learn how to dance and not just the Texas Two Step.

Chapter Three:
Creativity, Global Education and
Cultural Awareness the REEL World

"Your ability to act on your imagination is going to be so decisive in driving your future and the standard of living of your country. So the school, the state, the country that empowers, nurtures, enables imagination among its students and citizens, that's who's going to be the winner"

—Thomas L. Friedman

Teaching For Creativity

Not only is it important to be educated in generating ideas, it is even more important to develop skills in perception, analysis and creative thinking. When German engineer George Mestral was on an outdoor trip in the 1940's, he noticed that some thistles were attached to his clothes and dog fur. His curiosity peaked, and with some research, he found out these thistles had hooks that effectively attached to clothing, fur and hair. After developing that concept from nature into a product, Velcro was created and is regarded as one of the most important inventions of the century.

Students entering school today will be retiring around the year 2067. We have no idea of what the world will look in five years, much less sixty years, yet educators are charged with preparing our students for life in that world. Many will be working in jobs that have yet to be invented. Many will change their career directions several times before retiring. The need to learn and relearn is critical to their success. Their ability to find creative solutions to world problems is vital for all of us. Our students are facing many emerging issues such as global warming, famine, poverty, health issues, a global population explosion and other environmental and social issues. These issues lead to a need for students to be able to communicate, function and create change personally, socially, economically and politically on local, national and global levels.

Emerging technologies and resulting globalization also provide unlimited possibilities for exciting new discoveries and developments such as new forms of energy, medical advances, environmental solutions, communications, and exploration into space and into the depths of the oceans. The possibilities are unlimited but do our children have the creative abilities to meet the challenges ahead of them?

> "If we are to prepare successfully for the Twenty First Century we will have to do more than just improve literacy and numeration skills. We need a broad, flexible and motivating education that recognises the different talents of all children and delivers excellence to everyone."
>
> —White Paper Excellence in Schools, 1997 UK

The word creativity is used in different ways and in different contexts. For the purpose of this book the definition, as outlined by Ken Robinson in his book "Out of Our Minds," best describes the qualities required for deep creative thinking. The definition has four definite and measurable points. First, creativity involves the use of an imaginative process and engages a wide range of idea creation techniques such as brainstorming. Through the use of imagination the learner attempts to expand the possibilities of a given situation, to look at it from a fresh perspective, to see alternatives, to make unusual connections and to see relationships. Existing ideas may be combined, reinterpreted or applied in unexpected ways. Second, the ideas are directed toward achieving an objective. These ideas have a purpose or a reason. The action plan is in pursuit of the objective. The objective may change as new ideas and possibilities come to light, therefore, redefining the objective. Third, the process must create something that is original in concept. The originality of the idea may be unique to the individual or to his peer group. Fourth, the outcome must be of value in connection to the objective. It should be effective, useful, valid and tenable in terms of the objective. Therefore, creativity is an activity that uses the imagination to produce outcomes that are original and of value.

Creativity involves playing with ideas and trying out the possibilities. It can be a short term or a long term, cyclical process of small steps coupled with real world limits. Students must develop the ability to elaborate, analyse and evaluate their own ideas in order to make adjustments in their thinking and to improve. Opportunities need to be provided throughout the creative process that gives students the chance to communicate new ideas with others.

Creativity is not something that is restricted to the arts. It is possible for people to use creativity in all areas of human activity, including the arts, science, mathematics, humanities, at work, at play and throughout our daily lives. All people have the unique capabilities to be creative. For many students who struggle in traditional subject areas that involve literacy and mathematics, finding their creative strengths can often have a huge impact on their self-esteem and overall achievement.

"All human beings are born with unique gifts. The healthy functioning of our community depends on its capacity to develop each gift."

—Peter Senge, The Learning School

Highly creative people in all walks of life are often driven by a strong belief in their abilities within their chosen field. A positive self-belief is critical to their performance. The same holds true for our learners. Students need to be encouraged to believe in their creative potential, to engage their sense of possibility and to develop the confidence to be risk-takers. For this to begin to take place, a positive and supportive school culture must be established for all students. A learning environment must be developed where creativity is valued, where students are expected to and rewarded for going beyond subject expectations, where opportunities are provided for students to find personal relevance in the learning activities, where students explore and examine alternative ways of doing and showing knowledge and where the curriculum is balanced between learning content and skills and the freedom to innovate and experiment.

Creativity does not just happen in our classrooms. Teachers have to plan for it. They need to know not only what they are promoting, but also how to create opportunities for this to happen. There are many strategies that can be used to facilitate creative thinking, however, there is a clear distinction between teaching creatively and teaching for creativity. Creative teaching means using imaginative approaches to make learning exciting and interesting. A variety of teaching tools, strategies, resources and materials may be employed to encourage motivation and interest. This is a requirement for good teaching. Teaching for creativity involves the learner directly in the creative process and is intended to develop creative thinking and behaviour. The teacher creates an atmosphere where the creative abilities of all those in the classroom are engaged, student and teacher alike.

Ken Robinson, in his book "Out of Our Minds", describes three elements required when teaching for creativity: encouraging, identifying and fostering.

Encouraging students to believe in themselves as creative learners begins with helping learners to develop a positive attitude while rewarding them for risk taking, independence, persistence and resilience. Teaching for creativity involves helping students identify their own "special" talents and creative abilities. Students need to be given the opportunity to develop an understanding of themselves as creative learners. They must be encouraged to discover their unique learning styles and explore different ways of showing their understanding. Teachers need to help students become aware of what is involved in the creative process by fostering opportunities for students to take risks, make mistakes, role play and take on new challenges in an atmosphere of trust.

> "Each child has a spark in him/her. It is the responsibility of the people and institutions around each child to find what ignites that spark."
>
> —Howard Gardiner

Teaching for creativity should encourage students to be open to new and unusual ideas and to a variety of methods and approaches that emerge throughout the creative process. In doing so, students develop a respect for each other and for the uniqueness of their contributions. They learn the importance of suspending judgement and withholding decisions until all factors are considered. Throughout the process a creative relationship or bond is often created among the participants as a feeling of anticipation, satisfaction, enjoyment and involvement develops. A relationship among students and teachers must be established and maintained. Teaching for creativity encourages self-confidence, risk taking and independent thinking. The aim is for our students to become more effective in handling future problems, to develop a deeper understanding of themselves and the world around them and to be more accepting and open to the opinions of others.

Throughout the learning process, students need to be encouraged to self monitor and reflect upon their performances and progress. A sense of responsibility for learning is enhanced when students are asked to think about their thinking. Having students write a metacognition piece about how they are thinking fosters deeper ownership for the learning and helps them develop a capacity for goal setting and planning, self-assessment and self-management. To become successful lifetime learners, it is imperative that students become creative thinkers and develop a deep understanding of how they learn.

> "The ability to think about your own thinking (metacognition) is essential in a world of continuous change."
>
> —John Abbott

There is much concern among educators about the effectiveness of "new" methods of teaching and, in particular, the need to maintain rigour and authority in school. Many argue that once we stray from the path of formal education and move into the areas of exploratory learning, team work, project based learning and learning from experiences that promote creativity and self-expression, we are lowering the standards and reducing the opportunity for students to acquire necessary skills. The argument appears to surround the "either /or" theory of education, either core or exploratory. Good teaching to some is associated with formal instruction of specific skills and content. Creativity is viewed as an add-on activity reserved for "special" moments after the content material has been covered. Both ways of teaching are viewed as separate entities with no obvious connections.

Teaching the learner in the 21st century should involve a balance between formal instruction of content and of skills as well as giving our students the freedom to inquire, question, experiment and to express their own thoughts and ideas. The balance is a matter of extreme importance and necessary. The creative thinking process builds upon a student's grasp of the basic concepts. For example a young pianist cannot compose a song without having basic skills in playing the piano. These beginning skills cannot, nor should not be acquired through discovery. Many skills must be formally taught and practised. Genuine creative achievement draws from skills, knowledge and understanding that are often taught through formal instruction. Formal teaching strategies, alone, will not necessarily promote creative thinking. Opportunities must be provided for students to develop their creative thinking skills. A balance is required between teaching content and providing opportunities for innovation and experimentation.

> "The most important developments in civilization have come through the creative process, but ironically, most people have not been taught to create."
> —Robert Frotz, The Path of Least Resistance, 1994

Teaching with creativity and teaching for creativity involve many good teaching characteristics. Creative teachers know their curriculum very well and have a deep understanding of the ideas and principles within their subject areas. They have a grasp of the essential learning that students require to meet success in that subject area. Good teachers motivate and inspire their students through their personal passion for the subject. They have high standards and expectations and the ability to communicate openly with their students. They provide on-going differentiation of instruction and assessment to meet the individual needs of each learner. Good teaching skills are imperative for good learning but creative teachers need more than this. They also need strategies that stimulate curiosity and increase self-esteem and confidence in the learner. Opportunities need to be provided for the learners to help them make connections to prior understanding and to make new connections. Good teaching balances structured learning with relevant experiences that generate self-direction and personal understanding.

Good teachers ask quality questions designed to stimulate creativity and interest. Learning increases when students are presented with a balance between open and closed questions. Closed questions usually involve one answer or solution, whereas open questions can generate many different options. Too often teachers use closed questioning, with a reliance on linear processes and logical reasoning, as a primary source for learning. There is a definite time and place for such learning, but in many cases, this technique stifles creativity. Open questions offer greater opportunity for creative activity for the learner. One of the most powerful prompts a creative teacher can use begins with the words, "What if?" Questions beginning with these words often generate many answers and although some are better than others, none are completely wrong. Effective learning involves a blend of both types of questions.

> "One can't believe impossible things."
>
> "I daresay you haven't had much practice," said the Queen. "When I was your age I always did it for half-an-hour a day. Why, sometimes I've believed as many as six impossible things before breakfast."
>
> —Lewis Carroll, Alice's Adventures in Wonderland

Critical Thinking

> "Critical literacy has a rich history in development of
> education settings. From John Dewey to Lev Vygotsky
> to Paulo Freire, progressive education has been based
> on providing students not merely with functional skills,
> but with the conceptual tools necessary to critique and
> engage society along with its inequalities and injustices.
> Horace Mann, known as the Father of the Common
> School and free public education, challenged his stu-
> dents to, 'Be ashamed to die until you have won some
> victory for humanity.'"

—Patrick Shannon (1990), Professor of Education at
Pennsylvania State University

Critical thinking is the thought process used when exploring
and investigating complex questions and issues. The quality of
this reflective process is dependent on many factors such as:

The personal commitment to the topic being explored, and an
understanding of not just "what" is being learned but also "why";

The depth of understanding about the subject and the availability of relevant information;

What is known about the inquiry process, including asking
key questions and the strategies to answer questions, solve problems or issues;

The awareness that knowledge is "constructed" and therefore
judgement needs to be suspended until all viewpoints and factors
are considered;

The depth of understanding of the assumptions being made,
including prejudices, stereotypes, biases and distortions;

The knowledge of how information can be distorted and
manipulated to maintain a particular point of view;

The organization and monitoring of the inquiry process through feedback;

The value placed on other viewpoints and the flexibility to change when faced with "better" reasoning;

The awareness of the implications that may follow a decision and associated actions

> "...students' ability and willingness to think critically are most likely to develop when knowledge acquisition and thinking about content are intertwined rather than sequential."
>
> —Joanne Gainen Kurfiss, Santa Clara University

Critical thinking skills involve getting students to ask and answer questions about a subject or issue while they are acquiring an understanding. Open-ended questions invite curiosity about the topic and should "hook" the learner into the learning experience. Often students will try to answer these questions using their own personal connections but soon find out that their knowledge is not deep enough and further inquiry is required. It is the power of "needing to know more" that provides the fuel for critical thinking. The availability of resources allows the learner to further explore the topic, while judging the validity, quality and relevance of the information. Class discussions provide the students the opportunity to debate and clarify their understanding while developing knowledge of the subject, problem or issue.

> "Good questions work on us, we don't work on them. They are not a project to be completed but a doorway opening onto greater depth of understanding, actions that will take us into being more fully alive."
>
> —Peter Block

Providing students with a deep understanding of the complexity of critical thinking is a crucial factor in developing this skill. The critical thinking process must be clearly defined and formally taught. The knowledge of the stages of critical thinking and the many factors involved will provide both teachers and learners with the understanding of where they are in the development of the skill. The awareness of the process helps the learners understand the next step for growth and gives the teachers the guidance for what opportunities and learning experiences must be provided to ensure that growth takes place.

Global Education and Cultural Awareness

"Education makes us free....It is through education that we are liberated from powerlessness, from the burden of mistrust directed against ourselves. The individual who has been liberated from self-doubt, who has learned to trust him – or herself, is naturally able to believe in the latent capabilities of others. Education enables us to look beyond superficial difference to perceive the great earth, the great sea of life that sustains us all."

—Daisaku Ikeda, Bubbist Leader, New Delhi, October, 1997

Global education involves the awareness of problems and issues which go beyond borders. It is about the interconnectedness of systems throughout the world, cultural, ecological, economics, political and technological. Cultural awareness is learning to understand and appreciate those around us who have different cultural backgrounds, seeing the world through the eyes and minds of others and realizing that the wants and needs of the citizens of the world are much the same as ours.

Much like creative thinking, global education and cultural

awareness are often not viewed as curriculum. Teachers find it difficult to integrate global ideas into their lessons due largely to the excessive and restrictive demands of the current curriculum, which seem to leave no leeway to set up, manage and implement innovative teaching. Very little time is dedicated to providing learning experiences in this area. Some teachers attempt to address global perspectives but are often frustrated by lack of time and resources.

Globalization has had a huge impact, both economic and social. Although the economic growth rate has increased significantly over the last few years, so have economic inequalities widened at the same pace. Twenty percent of the world's wealthiest population in 1960 had 30 times more wealth than the poorest 20 percent: in 1997, that number rose, giving 74 times more income than the poorest, (UNDP, 1999). The rich are getting richer. With this comes an unequal distribution of resource consumption. The wealthiest nations of the world are consuming significantly more than their share of the available resources. Over consumption of resources also leads to huge environmental concerns due largely to increased waste and emissions. The United States for example, having only 5 percent of the total world population, causes over 30 percent of global emissions. An abuse of consumption and the environment is of major concern to all citizens of the world, however, those who contribute the least pay the highest cost for this damage, that being the poor.

People are beginning to realize that they can no longer see themselves as separate entities and instead must view themselves as global citizens with rights and responsibilities at the personal, national and world levels. Many are becoming aware of the consequences of the actions of a few and the need for world-wide solutions to ensure the survival of our planet. Students in the 21st century have to be "educated" to ask the right questions, to solve problems, to find creative solutions and to put a plan into action.

"America's classrooms are no place for mediocrity. Time for a generation to rise up, passionate people who care more about results than a pension and a pay check. It's time for the "pension and a pay check" people to CHECK OUT of education."

—Teacher Talks: Facebook

The challenge of preparing future citizens for the 21st century who can meet the demands of the new global realities is in the hands of today's educators. If students are to reach their full potential, educational goals must go beyond core subjects, instructional objectives and include values and expectations that help students understand the interconnectedness of all cultures and people. The 21st century is a world of globalization. This means that people from all parts of the world, whether through technological discoveries or issues of global concern, need one another in order to survive and prosper. The social and economic barriers of yesterday have been levelled and the playing field is open to all. Employers all over the world are looking for the most competent, most creative, most collaborative and most innovative people they can find and the talent pool is open to the world. Nations are working collaboratively seeking creative solutions to many global issues such as overpopulation, ecology and world health. Due to this interconnectedness, individuals need to redefine how they see themselves, their nation, their world and their place in it. Not only is it important to be aware of different cultures, societies and ethnic groups and this understanding relates to a global economy without borders, the citizen in the 21st century will also be expected to make a positive contribution. The question is how can this be done within our schools today? How do we help today's learners become cognizant of other peoples' well-being? How do we help them understand the growing and complex needs that surround them and how do we have them internalize the need for respect of cultural diversity?

Many changes are ahead of us if we are to meet the needs of our planet and find solutions to the serious problems facing our existence. The citizens in the 21st century must look beyond their borders to witness humanity as a whole. Education is a key factor to bringing about this change. Teachers have the power to cultivate understanding, challenge the status quo and encourage new ways of thinking. The learning environment we create in our classrooms can help students understand their cultural values and become accepting of the cultures of others. The better students understand their relationships with peers, family, community and nation, the better they will comprehend their role as global citizens. It is very important that students in the 21st century learn to move beyond passive acceptance of what exists, to an active desire to create a change by exploring that which can exist.

> "We stand at a critical moment in Earth's history, a time when humanity must choose it's future. As the world becomes increasingly interdependent and fragile, the future at once holds great peril and great promise. To move forward one must recognize that in the midst of a magnificent diversity of cultures and life forms we are one human family and one Earth community with a common destiny. We must join together to bring forth a sustainable global society founded on respect for nature, universal human rights, economic justice, and a culture of peace. Towards this end, it is imperative that we, the peoples of Earth, declare our responsibility to one another, to the greater community of life and to future generations."
>
> —Earth Charter Preamble, 2000

The process of developing global awareness and cultural diversity begins with the teacher. The teacher's knowledge and attitude sets the stage for acceptance. Teachers need to ask themselves why they teach and what education is all about. There has to be so much more to education than what lies inside a textbook. Teachers are more than just a source of content information. They have the power to shape young minds and build a better tomorrow. Teachers need to view education as a way to foster understanding and acceptance of others.

Paolo Freire, Brazilian educator, states that teachers must share their knowledge and experiences. He continues to say that teachers should also create an environment for learners to realize their vast unlimited potential so they can creatively build their own future. The traditional approach of filling the minds of students with facts and information does nothing to promote global awareness. Instead, students need experience in critical thinking, in taking part in cross-cultural experiences and to making well thought out decisions that can be sustainable. Students have to be taught to think for themselves, suspend judgement and defend their opinions. Freire defines the traditional teaching method as the "banking system." He calls this the "oppressed" way of teaching where students have no voice. He continues to argue for an alternative approach that is flexible and allows the students to participate in their learning experiences, calling this "transformative teaching." Teachers can motivate and inspire their students while helping them find meaning and purpose in life. Give the students the experience to develop a voice and opportunities to be heard.

> "What I can and ought to do is to challenge the students to perceive their experience of learning, the experience of being a subject capable of knowing. My role as a progressive teacher is helping the student to recognize themselves as the architects of their own cognitive process."
>
> —Paolo Freire

The first step towards global awareness begins by shaping attitudes. As was the case with teaching for creativity, good learning requires good teaching. An atmosphere of belonging, respect and caring is an important part of developing a healthy attitude in the learner. The power of the teacher can never be underestimated. The actions displayed by the teacher acts as a model for the learner. Good teachers actively show acceptance of everyone in their classrooms.

On a daily basis, teachers face the challenges of recognizing their students as unique individuals. Some students struggle with the academic material, others suffer from lack of social skills or simply have trouble believing in themselves. All students learn differently and show their understanding in ways that are unique to them. Some come from rich learning environments at home while others have little to no guidance beyond school. Regardless of the student's background, personal history, strengths or weaknesses, teachers have the responsibility to support and nurture students, while respecting their uniqueness and creating a "global" sense of belonging in each student. Cultural acceptance begins in the classroom. It involves accepting the uniqueness of those around us. Only when the learners have developed this level of acceptance will they be able to move towards the acceptance of others. Teachers must act as models of acceptance and acknowledge diversity openly in their classrooms.

> "We can learn a great deal from the very students we teach. For this to happen it is necessary that we transcend the monotonous arrogant, and elitist traditionalism where the teacher knows all and the student does not know anything."
>
> —Freire, Paulo (1985). Rethinking critical pedagogy: A dialogue with Paulo Freire. The politics of education: Culture, power and liberation

Effective teachers not only try to show their acceptance of each student in their class, they also attempt to create opportunities for learners to recognize their unlimited potential. Respect for each student comes from the realization and understanding that each student is in a continuous state of development. Freire refers to this as a state of "unfinishedness" (1998). Once teachers recognize that students are not complete when they enter our classes, they begin to show true respect for each learner. Teachers are a part of the student's development. They help them move forward. Treating students with respect for who they are and where they are at acts as a catalyst for independent thinking and understanding. The respect that students sense from their teachers empowers them to feel important and confident about themselves. It often motivates them to do well. It is a vital contributing factor to student growth. It is through this display of respect that students begin to feel that they are valued and can make a difference, not just in their school or community but also in the world. This modelling of respect guides students to treat others around them with the same kind of respect given to them. Showing respect is important for the building of a positive teacher-student relationship. When students see or feel that their teachers respect them, they also feel that their teachers care for them and that all things are possible. All people feel inspired and empowered when feeling supported and respected.

> "..a successful classroom is a place where each student feels that indeed they have a place; a place, over time, where relationships can be trusted, where inner dreams as well as demons can be shared without ridicule by both teacher and students alike, where individual differences of colour, creed and origin are seen as contributive to a shared future."
>
> —Smith, D. (2000). A Few Modest Prophecies: The WTO, Globalization, and the Future of Public Education. Canadian Social Studies

As educators we need to help our students make connections with the world around them. A West African proverb says, "The world is like a Mask dancing; we cannot see it if we stand in one place". Teachers must broaden their understanding of teaching and become knowledgeable of ways of providing learning opportunities for their students. We need to instil in our students curiosity of the world and a desire to work together in making our world a better place. We need to create an environment where different cultures can learn to respect each other's way of looking at the world, where all opinions are respected and valued. We just have to look at things from a difference place.

> "I imagine a school system that recognizes learning is natural, that a love of learning is normal, and that real learning is passionate learning. A school curriculum that values questions above answer...creativity above fact regurgitation...individuality above conformity...and excellence above standardized performance...And we must reject all notions of 'reform' that serve up more of the same: more testing, more 'standards', more uniformity, more conformity, more bureaucracy."
>
> —Tom Peters Author 'Re-imagine'

Chapter Four:
Technology and the 21st Century Learner

John Milton Fogg in his book, "The Greatest Networker in the World", tells the story of a young monk who was seeking wisdom from a wise and old master. The two met and shared a conversation over a cup of tea. The older monk, while listening to the young man boast of his great talents and knowledge, poured a cup of tea and allowed it to spill into the lap of his guest. As the master continued to calmly pour the tea, which had over-filled the students' cup, the young man asked why this was happening.

> "Go away from me, young man, the master said. I have nothing to teach you. Your cup is too full, overflowing with all that you know and all that you think you don't know. Come back to me when your cup is empty and you are ready to receive what I have to give."
>
> —John Milton Fogg, The Greatest Networker in the World, The Secret Revealed

The lesson to be learned is that for people to move forward they must open their minds to what is new. The secret is in knowing that there are things you don't know. Growth for teachers involves an understanding that there is much to learn. Once becoming aware that there is much to learn, steps must be taken to acquire that knowledge.

Like the teacup story, in order to learn, we have to be humble, to empty our minds and to make room for the new. The secret of great teaching comes not from what you know but from the wisdom of knowing what you don't know and doing something about it. Great teachers are great learners, their unquenchable appetite for knowledge is never satisfied. They welcome new ideas, new strategies and new challenges with open arms and embrace the moment with excitement and enthusiasm.

Many teachers prepare to teach by simply learning the subject that they will teach and the methods and strategies of teaching that subject. "Most teachers forget that teaching is an art." (James M Banner Jr. And Harold C. Cannon: The Elements of Teaching 1999) In the book, "How We Think" John Dewey discusses the claim that the true teacher is an artist. Dewey asks the question, "What does it takes for a teacher to be an artist?" Dewey's answer to the question lies not just in the kind actions a teacher takes to create energy and enthusiasm, but also in the way in which the tools at the teacher's disposal are connected with subject objectives and successfully carried into action. Teaching becomes a true art form when teachers go beyond mere technical skills in the way they use means and materials and, more importantly, in the way the "educative experience" connects with the learner.

> "The artists are different. They took a leap. They weren't pushed. They jumped."
>
> —Seth Godin

Dewey sees the students as active participants in the learning process. The teacher's task is to bring the students into a learning experience, making them engaged problem solvers. The difficulty for the teacher is to find out what is a meaningful educative experience for the students. What the teacher regards as an interesting area for exploration, may not be viewed in the same way by the students. The key to being the "artist" is to make connections to the learners, engaging them with methods that apply to their world, their means of understanding and their ways of communicating.

> "When attention to means is inspired by recognition of the ends they serve, we have the attitude typical of the artist, an attitude that may be displayed in all activities, even though not conventionally designated arts."
>
> —John Dewey: How We Think 1910

Growing up in the sixties, in a small town in eastern Ontario, provided me with few opportunities to explore the world beyond my own experiences. What I knew about the world came to me from listening to my parents, watching television, listening to the radio and talking with my friends. My teachers provided me with the opportunity to develop the skills I needed to move from intellectual darkness to illuminated awareness. School was an empowering experience as it exposed many of us, for the first time, to a wide variety of experiences that we had never thought about nor could have discovered on our own. The way we connected to the world around us was carefully guided by what we were taught and our means of making these connections were very limited. Teachers were the people who showed us the "light." They owned the knowledge and parcelled it out grade by grade, subject by subject.

In the 21ˢᵗ century, students grow up in the" light."(Marc Prensky) They are deeply exposed to the world long before they come to school. The students today are connected to the world twenty four hours a day and in real time. Technology is in the blood of today's teenagers. They are born "digital natives". Marc Prensky in his book, Turning on the Lights, (2008) claims that students are born in the light, "from the first flash of the camera at the moment of birth, [...students] arrive at school full of knowledge, thoughts, ideas and opinions about their world and their universe." They continue to define their world through television, movies, rock videos, interactive animations and games, cell phones, chat lines, blogs, twitters, facebook, instant messaging, emails and the internet. The learners today can explore the universe completely on their own without the guidance of a teacher. They share their views of the world with each other and often have their opinions and views reinforced by other self discoverers. Through technology, students are growing up knowing about or being able to find out about anything they want, good or bad. Their exposure to the world is neither guided nor filtered.

> "Schools are struggling to keep pace with the astonishing rate of change in student's lives outside of school. Students will spend their adult lives multitasking, in a multifaceted, technology-driven, diverse vibrant world - and they must arrive equipped to do so."
>
> —Partnership for 21st Century Skills

It would make perfect sense that knowing this, educators would be embracing the technology available and using it to build upon and strengthen the students' engagement in the learning process. Instead, many schools block student access to the world by implementing internet filters, banning the use of cell phones and cell phone cameras, blocking instant messaging, student emails, Wikipedia, and other potentially effective educational tools and technologies. Many schools have decided that all the "light" that surrounds the students, their electronic connections to the world, is somehow detrimental to their education. As a result schools systematically tell the students, as they enter the school, to shut off all their connections. The restrictions placed on technology in an effort to protect students may be doing more harm than good and the learning of the 21st century student could be greatly affected. Prensky quotes a teenage boy as saying he has to "power down" when he gets to school, in a literal and intellectual way. It is acknowledged that there is much more to this issue than simply allowing students to use technology in the school environment.

Not all technology can be used for effective learning. There must be an educational value behind the use of any tool. Using cell phones, podcasting or instant messaging as a simple form of communication serves little purpose in developing 21st century skills. Using these tools to allow students to share information and collaborate on group projects provides a learning experience that is reinforced by the technology. Teachers must help students learn to use technology effectively and respectfully. There will always be attempts to abuse the use of technology and therefore it is very important that students be taught technology etiquette. Along with the privilege of using tools of the 21st century, comes responsibility for using it properly.

> "A powerful vision of public education is critical for closing the gap between how students live and how they learn in school. Students who have access to technology outside school will find schools without access to and integration of technology into their course work to be antiquated and irrelevant to their world."
>
> —Partnership for 21st Century Skills

That is not to say that technology is not being used in our schools, however, the way it is used is mostly to reinforce what we have always done but now it is in digital format. When a new technology appears, the instinct is to continue to do things within the technology the way it was always done. Educators use it to pass documents and information around in the same way they always did but now it is in an electronic format and the result is not very different from the way it was. Writing, submitting and sharing work digitally on the computer is still just a new way of doing old things. Having students use the internet to research a topic, word processing for composition and power point for presentation is nothing more than upgrading tools and resources. The use of an LCD projector or Smart Board is just a step up from the overhead projector if what it is being used for is to present old things in a new way. Are we moving the learner into the 21st century with progressive education? How can technology be used to develop and reinforce skills that will be required beyond school?

Web 2.0

Web 2.0 or Web is a frequently used term that describes a new generation of websites. The expression implies that the early internet websites, referred to as Web 1.0, were much different than that of the newer version. The initial use of the internet was for accessing fixed information, that is, material that was downloaded or forwarded to the internet user. Web 2.0 is different in the sense that is more participatory, dynamic and social in its design and use. It involves uploading for the purpose of communicating and collaborating. Web 2.0 actively encourages engagement and interaction.

> Web 2.0 is defined as an online application that uses the World Wide Web (www) as a platform and allows for participatory involvement, collaboration, and interactions among users. Web 2.0 is also characterized by the creation and sharing of intellectual and social resources by end users.
>
> —Leadership for Web 2.0 in Education: Promise and Reality, Cheryl Lemke, Ed Coughlin, COSN (2009)

Early websites typically allowed the users to download content from the associated pages, along with any connected multi-media files. Presently sites such as flickr, You Tube and many others only exist because the users want to upload and share pictures, videos or other multi-media files. In addition to sharing files, the Web 2.0 user can also write into existing web pages that are published on line. Other Web 2.0 tools involve weblogs and wikis.

Weblogs or blogs are usually a collaborative space for users to write short pieces on an ongoing basis. Professional and amateur journalists have used blogs to publish breaking news. Comments allow readers to offer feedback on each entry. In school blogging has many potential uses. Blogs can be used by students to organize thoughts and ideas. They can be used as a way to reflect on learning experiences. Students may use blogs to keep useful links, video, photos and materials for themselves or to share with others. Group blogs can be used as a communication tool for small teams and group work outside the classroom. Blogs can also promote online discussion and collaboration. Because a blog is owned by its author and monitored by the teacher, it can promote safe personal communication and networking.

Wikis are collaborative websites which allows many authors to work together to create, edit and comment on the content. One of the best known wikis is Wikipedia. Wikipedia is an online encyclopedia based on contributions from others. Classroom wikis can be safeguarded by a password. Wikis are a great medium for creating, collecting and refining group knowledge. A class or small group of students can create a wikis on any topic, or on any subject. The teacher can monitor the additions and changes made by students. Like other media, wikis are available online, at school and from home and are available 24 hours a day.

With the explosion of new material and websites, comes an increase in the number of people using the internet. This has resulted in the development of many interactive, user friendly, websites which have led to a huge mass of users sharing common interests. The internet has become a source of community-building, involving people from all corners of the world. Online, social networking has become a platform for facilitating and developing relationships, old and new. Increased internet involvement has resulted in a richer online environment with a wealth of media material to share.

Trent Batson, university professor, writer and communication strategist argues in his online article, "Why is Web 2.0 Important to Higher Education?" that Web 2.0 technologies have "...created a landscape of learning – collaborative, problem based, experiential - that is closer to our nature than ranked, single voice classrooms so abundant in recent times." Batson points out that the learning tools, being used by imaginative teachers in the 21st century, are not print-based but rather communication directed. The conversations in classrooms have become more valuable than the knowledge of the lecturer. The new textbook for the 21st century, according to Batson, will be the work the students generate under the guidance of their teachers.

> "Culturally speaking, with the advent of Web 2.0, the traditional classroom with one speaker and many listeners is now an oddity, a throwback, a form that should represent 15 percent of undergraduate interaction with faculty, not 85 percent as it does now. With so many ways to create knowledge now very rapidly and collaboratively, we are freed from the necessity of a singular approach to teaching."
>
> —Trent Batson, Why is Web 2.0 Important to Higher Education?(2009)

Many creative teachers and engaged students are encouraging the use of Web 2.0 technologies in schools but human and technological barriers are holding back the use of these tools in classrooms. A recent study (2009) was conducted by Interactive Educational Systems Design Inc, an independent educational research company, to examine the current status, future plans and challenges for using Web 2.0 technologies in K-12 schools. The study was commissioned by Lightspeed Systems and Thinkonize Inc., a company that created a student search engine called net-Trekker. According to the survey, the top 3 reasons school districts are using Web 2.0 technologies are to address students' individual learning needs, engage students' interest and increase students' options for access to teaching and learning. What is also important to note from the study is that school districts throughout North America are at many different stages of use and adoption of Web 2.0 technologies.

The study lists some of the technologies being used in schools today. Online communication tools and digital multi-media resources rank as the most commonly used. Very few teachers use online social networking as part of their instruction. The reasons for this, as reported in the study, were lack of teacher knowledge about how to use social networking effectively and teachers' perception that it has little instructional value. The most frequently cited concerns were about monitoring student safety and protecting against misuse. The question remains, "Should these fears and insecurities, on behalf of teachers, contribute to outmoded teaching practices?" It is important to recognize teachers' concerns, while at the same time providing students with the type of learning environment which is relevant to them as learners. The responsibility for ensuring safe internet use lay with both the teachers and the website providers. There is no shortage of products on the market that offer blogs, wikis, and even social networks that can be used in the classroom. Teachers must be open to using these products and the designers must ensure safety for both the educators and learners.

> "So much of what we hear is that schools are not implementing social networking tools. This is because a lot of districts hear this and think Facebook or MySpace. It doesn't have to be like that."
>
> —Paul Kuhne, Vice President of Marketing, eChalk

Many companies which develop social networking tools for online use have created programs that are pass-word protected for teachers and students. Programs are available that can be used for a specific school, a certain classroom or just one small group. These companies are recognizing the importance of finding solutions that guarantee safety for use in schools.

The Consortium for School Networking (CoSN) conducted a study to look at the gap between how students learn in school and how they interact outside of school. The CoSN research reveals that although 77 percent of district administrators in the study agreed with the importance of Web 2.0 as a teaching and learning tool, most still ban online social networking and chat rooms in their schools.

According to the CoSN study the seven highest ranking priorities for Web 2.0 use by district administrators were:

1. Keeping students interested and engaged in school

2. Meeting the needs of different kinds of learners

3. Developing critical thinking skills

4. Developing capabilities in students that can't be acquired through traditional methods

5. Providing alternative learning environments for students

6. Extending learning beyond the school day

7. Preparing students to be lifelong learners

Web 2.0 tools can provide highly interactive learning experiences for the learners. Uploading and web page editing has generated new forms of internet participation for students. Search engines such as Google and Yahoo, which include in their internet searches material uploaded by users, encourage the exchange of information in the form of sounds, pictures and video files. With this vast amount of available information comes the need for students to be able check the validity of the material they are viewing. Alan November, founder and senior partner of November Learning, points out that children often use the internet without being taught how to use it. There are many sites available to check the reliability of websites. Students must be taught how to evaluate the quality of the information they are accessing and the appropriateness of that information. Alan November, at novemberlearning.com, provides many valuable links to these sites.

> "The fact remains that kids will increasingly depend on the Internet for information. As they use the Web, they need to evaluate their findings using several techniques."
> —Alan November

Technology Dominates

It all begins, once again, with the teacher. Teachers' openness to change, their attitude towards learning and their understanding of the role as educators is the foundation for the future of our students. Teachers must challenge themselves to operate outside their comfort zones and to grow as professionals. Fighting the natural evolution of change and technology is about as worthwhile as arguing with teenagers about pop music. As teachers, we are denying our students a valuable learning experience if we do not include the technological component as part of our teaching equation. When used wisely, technology can be a great learning tool, however, technology by itself does not replace a great teacher, it augments a great teacher. Good teaching is always maintained by employing an "artistic" balance between what we know and what we need to know, specifically combining what we know about education with what we need to know about technology.

> "Technology is a vehicle, not a destination...rather aspects of technology – like all components of an effective course – should be chosen according to how they help meet the learning objectives."
>
> —Jim Henry, Jeff Meadows,Nine Principles for Excellence in Web Based Teaching

Technology is here to stay and it is only going to become more pervasive and central to the way we communicate. Everyday our lives become increasing more connected to technology. Students must be prepared, not only to use technology, but to learn how to use it to produce the best results. Technology must be viewed as a tool that will further develop students' understanding and assists them with the sharing of their knowledge.

Technology, and specifically, information technology, is transforming the global economy and drastically changing the way business and society operates. There must be a corresponding change in our schools to ensure students have the necessary skills to meet with success in the digital age. Understanding how to use technology to locate and evaluate information, to learn, reason, make decisions, solve problems, and to collaborate and work in teams will be essential skills in the rapidly changing world. These are the 21st century skills that will be crucial for students to thrive in the digital age. Without a serious and significant investment in these skills, schools face the almost impossible challenge of trying to create 21st century learners for a 21st century workforce in 20th century educational environments.

The business world is changing rapidly as companies try to stay competitive in the new global economy. Electronic commerce is booming as many companies keep their heads above water by finding creative ways to use the internet to strengthen their relationships with employees, suppliers and customers. Successful businesses are finding ways to combine both internet services and personal contact. Routine transactions are left to the internet with the use of e-commerce, information and communications such as email, faxes, voice mail, are conducted online and face-to-face interaction is left for situations that will have the largest impact.

> "... different combinations of face-to-face, ear-to-ear and keyboard-to-keyboard. Each has its place. The internet doesn't replace people. It makes them more efficient. By moving routine interactions to the Web and enabling customers to do some things for themselves, we've freed up our salespeople to do more meaningful things with customers."
>
> —Michael Dell, Dell Computers

Bill Gate's 12th rule for business is to "use digital tools to help customers solve problems for themselves." Gates refers to this innovation as "Business at the Speed of Thought." He goes on to say that you know you have built an excellent "digital nervous system" when the information flows through an organization as quickly and naturally as thought in a human being. It can be argued that business does not represent education, and to some extent, that is true. It is, however, foolish to ignore what is happening beyond the walls of our schools.

Putting this into an educational context is very simple. Teachers have to do things differently if they are going to prepare citizens for the ways of the 21st century. Not just workers will need the skills for survival in the years ahead, so will consumers. The way we shop, communicate, obtain information, interact with people, file our taxes, everything is moving into the digital domain. Technology is not going away. Teachers have to embrace the power of this tool and use it to their and the students advantage.

There is always anxiety about using something that is unfamiliar and there are many excuses to avoid using new educational technologies. Statements such as, "I'm not a technical person," "I don't have the resources," "I don't know how," "I don't have time to learn something new," "That's not my job,"or "I have content material to cover," reinforces some teacher's lack of vision and an unwillingness to learn and grow professionally. Many teachers have a fear of technology and believe it cannot enhance learning, even when it seems inevitable that technology will be increasingly used in teaching and learning, just as it is in every other area of life. Computers will not replace good teachers, but teachers who use computers will inevitably replace teachers who do not.

Computers, at this point in time, will not replace teachers because they cannot do most of the personal things teachers do such as lesson planning, individual counselling, evaluation of process and product, meet with parents and so on. Teachers, in the near future, will most likely do the same things teachers do now but will use technology to provide a richer and more engaging learning environment. The change in education will come in the relationship between the student and the teacher. Teachers are going to have to give up some control as the students become more autonomous and active learners. The role of the teacher is changing from that of information holder to one of learning coach. Teachers will become less the providers of information and take on new roles as explainers, context providers, meaning makers and evaluators of information. There are huge changes ahead for teachers and education and the changes will be rapid and deep. Teachers must begin to prepare now for what is ahead of them. They must empty the tea cup and make room for the new.

To move forward in understanding, teachers need to learn to listen, to observe, to ask, and to try new methods their students have already figured out and use on a regular basis. They need to consult with students. They are far ahead of the "digital immigrants" in terms of taking advantage of digital technology.

Unfortunately, seldom do teachers ask students for their help. Imagine a curriculum designed with the teachers professional understanding of educational processes coupled with the student's knowledge of technology. Both student and teacher could provide a light for each to share.

Technology for Understanding and Understanding Technology

> "Rapid technological change, global competitive pressures and new patterns of work are demanding a more sophisticated set of transferable skills such as problem-solving, communication, decision-making, teamwork, leadership, entrepreneurship and adaptability."
>
> —State of Learning in Canada – Toward a Learning Future, Canadian Council of Learning

There is much more to integrating technology into classroom instruction than teaching computer skills and using specialized software in isolated situations. Effective technological integration must happen across the curriculum in ways that will deepen and enhance the learning experience. To have an impact on student learning, technology needs to be seamlessly woven into the curriculum is such a way that it becomes one of many tools being used to support the goals and objectives of the subject. Technology must be used to assist the teacher and learner in the learning process. Properly used, technology will help students acquire the skills to survive in a complex, highly technological knowledge based world. In the school environment technology should never be employed in total isolation. Gimmicks and passing fads, although tempting and potentially engaging, do nothing to enhance learning and will not, on their own, develop the skills of the 21st learner. The teacher, as an artist must skilfully mix and blend the colours on their palette to create the perfect picture.

Teachers are aware that the students in their classes have a variety of learning preferences and styles. They also know that learning improves when they involve students in experiences that engage and activate different senses such as visual, auditory, tactile and so on. The more we integrate into the learning experience, the better something is learned and the more easily it can be accessed again later. Computers and related technologies are excellent tools for accessing multi-sensory learning because they can provide sound, colour, graphics, animation and video in addition to written text. With technology, students can receive comprehensive, individualized instruction in many skill areas with frequent interaction and feedback, obtain a connection to the real world, while listening, reading and writing, all at the same time.

Many programs are designed to meet the specific needs of each learner by employing adaptive technology. Speech recognition technology, for example, allows students to record answers to questions and to compose essays at the command of their voice. Reading text and talking word processors help to engage struggling learners in the reading process. The computer has great potential to allow students to use the learning style that works best for them and to proceed through a program of study at their own pace, with immediate correction, explanation and reinforcement but again this cannot be used in isolation. Visual and auditory aids such as photographs, drawing, videos and sound provide the learner with a broader learning experience.

In the same way that teachers are aware that all students learn in ways that are unique and personal, it is also recognized that students show their understanding in a variety of unique ways as well. Not all students are capable of showing a deep understanding using a traditional pen and paper method. Technology can provide students with a multitude of opportunities to creatively display their knowledge and emotional connection to a topic. Through technology, students can openly communicate their feelings in ways that are unique to them. The power of communication and collaboration is deeply enhanced when students are given the chance to share their experiences with others in ways that are special to them.

The use of technology in the classroom can help educators refine their teaching practice and make learning a deeper and more lasting experience for students. Technology that is effectively integrated into the curriculum can build on the student's interests and extend those interests by having students communicating and collaborating with peers around the globe. The classroom can become a memorable learning environment where students reach out to their world and find their place in it.

> "Preparing students today for tomorrow's workforce has a lot to do with teaching about how to use and evaluate knowledge. The Internet is rapidly becoming the biggest repository of information we have ever known. The key will be in our ability to find, evaluate and use the information it provides. We need to teach analytical and organizational skills. Students must know how to evaluate data. Gone are the days when students spent their time memorizing facts that were readily available at their fingertips. Students need to learn communication and study skills. We must give them the type of tools that prepare them for lifelong learning, so they know how to study and how to evaluate the importance of what they learn."
>
> —Leight, M. Converge

Today's youth are more plugged in than any other generation before them. They do not view technology as a resource, it is simply an everyday part of their life. Technology is an extension of them as individuals and their personal way of connecting to the realities of their world. Blogs, wikis, text messages and podcasts are as common to them as picking up a telephone was to older generations. Never would my parents have considered the telephone as technology. Many students today are excellent self learners, often exploring the "new" without fear of failure. They teach themselves how to navigate complex games, how to use new computer programs and how to unlock the new technologies hidden inside a cell phone. They are extremely good at risk taking and trial and error to solve many technological mysteries. The 21st century learner navigates the internet with the speed of a formula one driver, while text messaging and communicating on Skype. They are masters of their own universe often without guidance. They are "seeing the light", forming their image of the world, without our guidance. As a result, they are not learning how to effectively use technology to help structure their learning in and out of school. Combine this with the naivety and vulnerability of youth and we have a problem of huge proportions. To ignore technology as a part of education is a mistake. The treacherous waters of the technological world are filled with sharks waiting to take advantage of anyone ignorant of the dangers.

The education system must provide experiences for students to engage positively with information technologies, to know how to use them and to enhance their creative thinking skills. New technologies are providing challenging opportunities for creative thinking and achievement and new ways to access ideas, information and people. Students must be able to see these new technologies as tools for creative achievement rather than ends in themselves. Secondly, students must be given the opportunity to explore the impact of new technologies on how they live, think and relate to one another. They need to be aware of the social and personal impact of technology. The internet is an extremely powerful tool with very few restrictions or limitations. Students have to be taught how to critically analyse information for its quality and value. Nothing from the internet can be taken on face value. It is critical that the 21st century citizen learns how to control technology rather than be controlled by it. They need to be shown the "light" to safely navigate the waters ahead of them.

> "Life is more than work. If we give children the idea that they need high level skills only for work, we have got it all wrong. They are going to need even higher-level skills to perform in a democratic society. We have got to get this absolutely right: the issue is not technology, but what it means to be human. What kind of future we want for the human race."
>
> —John Abbott, Why Good Schools Alone Will Never Be Enough

Beyond Technology – Beyond Content

In a world dominated by technology it would be too easy to assume that by equipping the 21st century learner with up-to-date technological skills that all would be well. These skills are important and will play a significant role in the lives of each citizen, but they are not enough. As global citizens, we must have a basic understanding of technology if we are to be active participants in the future ahead of us. The truly blessed will be those people who understand technology and can make it work to their advantage. Those who can put technology to work will have a definite advantage over those who are manipulated and controlled by its overwhelming presence.

The same holds true for those who believe that the skills currently being taught in the public system, with a focus on content material, will be a guarantee of success beyond secondary school. Many teachers believe it is their primary role to prepare students for educational experiences after high school. The reality is that many students in high school throughout North America do not attend post-secondary institutions let alone graduate from them.

According to an article which appeared in USA Today, entitled More People (2004), the U.S Census Bureau's Educational Attainment in the United States 2003 Study says only 27.2% of high school graduates 25 years of age and older had a bachelor's degree. The majority of our students are not graduating from university or college yet high schools are often dominated with courses which are directed towards the goal of post secondary education for all. Many schools are out of sync with the realities of the world beyond the classroom.

What is needed is a fundamental shift in the way teachers present material to students. An instructional approach that will provide students with the opportunity to develop real-world, problem-solving skills as well as giving students the content knowledge required to be an educated person. No one can successfully argue that specific content skills are not necessary for today's learners. The learner in the 21st century needs more than these skills. Acquiring facts and information for the sole purpose of passing or failing a test is futile. Students must be taught to look at the significance of that information, to be logical, to reason and make wise judgements about how all of this connects to their learning. The time has come to rethink how we teach students if we want to prepare them for the world that lies before them, time to discover the artist that lives in every teacher, time to recognize that we know that we don't know, time to empty our cups and begin to refill with a tea steeped with 21st century knowledge and understanding.

Globalization, changing demographics, economic restructuring, information technology and an increasing demand for training and retraining will also have a huge impact on the way students are educated at the post secondary level. To address the huge demands placed on existing institutions of higher education, new methods of delivering programs must be explored. James Morrison in an article entitled "U.S. Higher Education in Transition," suggests that by the year 2020 higher education throughout the world will look much different than it has in the past. A predominance of online courses has already begun to challenge the traditional method of instruction at several major campuses. Online education has become big business and has drawn the attention of major corporations around the world. It is predicted that many future college and university courses will be a combination of online and in-class instruction. Professors will no longer use lectures as a major source of instruction as project based learning becomes the norm. The focus of education will be to produce a graduate who can use a variety of information technology tools to access, evaluate, analyse, and communicate information and who can work effectively in teams with people from different ethnic backgrounds. The post-secondary institutions will produce students who can address real world issues, problem solve, collaborate with others globally and engage in continuous, self-directed learning.

> "The old hierarchical, geographically based university is dying. But progressive educators and innovative reformers are reviving the institution, using rapidly maturing information technologies and building upon timeless values of scholarship, collegiality, open dialogue and intellectual integrity to create a post-industrial university that will be capable of reaching both new heights of academic excellence and new breadths of community access and social utility."
>
> —James Morrison, U.S. Higher Education in Transition

Chapter Five:
A Paradigm Shift From Teaching to Learning

With the rate of information growth continuously accelerating, all levels of education, elementary through to university, must place less emphasis on the amount of memorization and repetition of material and more on making connections, thinking through issues, and solving problems. We must move beyond the old university model of asking students to absorb vast amounts of information. Even educators at the post secondary level are recognizing the need for change as they explore new learning experiences for their students. Learning is a life-long process of adjusting to constant change. Learning how to learn has become incredibly important. The content that is being taught to our students is not as significant as the manipulation of the content resources.

"'How can I get my students to think?' is a question asked by many faculty, regardless of their disciplines. Problem-based learning (PBL) is an instructional method that challenges students to 'learn to learn', work cooperatively in groups to seek solutions to real world problems. These problems are used to engage students' curiosity and initiate learning the subject matter. PBL prepares students to think critically and analytically, and to find and use appropriate learning resources."

—Barbara Duch

There are no teaching methods that can assure learning will occur, however, some methods are shown to do a better job of engaging students meaningfully with the subject matter. These methods place the students at the centre of the learning process. Opportunities need to be created for students to learn at a deep level, where they produce long-term understanding and are able to problem-solve using the concepts in new contexts. For learning to be engaging and enduring, the experiences must directly involve the student in the process. Deep learning only occurs when the student does the work. Students must question, make connections, organize information, and practice skills in order to further their own understanding. Many activities such as solving a problem, discussing and debating, role-playing, sharing understanding and conceptual mapping can be incorporated into a traditional method of teaching and will increase the student's chances of learning at a deep level, however, a teacher can get the best results when active learning strategies are combined with a teaching method that is designed on the basis of student engagement.

Educators must also be aware that the learning preference of the 21st century students is to work in teams and small groups with peer-to-peer interaction, in a structured environment with guidance and built in, flexibility. They have a need to be engaged in their learning and want to experience real life, first-hand learning opportunities that will allow them the freedom to explore something of value to them. They want to be challenged to reach their own conclusions and find their own results. They have a burning desire to make a difference in the world and need to explore their inner passions.

"An ounce of experience is worth a ton of theory."

—John Dewey

One of the core values of teaching and learning in the 21st century is to provide the students with opportunities to apply what they learn in real-world situations. The theoretical basis to this aim is that people learn and retain more when they see the relevance of what they are learning to their own lives. To bring meaning to real world experiences implies an understanding and awareness of the real world. One of the roles of schools is to give students a perspective of the society and the world they live in.

Traditional methods of teaching, such as the teacher lecturing to the students, often involved the delivery of as much information as possible and as quickly as possible. Many recent university graduates can relate to this model of instruction. The lecture method was a very effective and efficient way to deliver large amounts of information. This type of instruction offered little to no opportunity for student engagement, and as result, the learner assumed a passive role in the learning process, relying on note taking, memorization and repetition for learning.

> "As teachers, we tend to present material to our classes in the form of the results of our discipline's work. We collect the data, do the reading and synthesize the material into a finished product. Students, in their assignments and exams, are generally expected to demonstrate that they have learned what we as scholars have already found out. Rarely are they provided the opportunity to make those discoveries themselves. And yet it is potentially very rewarding to offer students the opportunity to use of raw materials themselves, giving them 'hand on' experience doing the work of the discipline."
>
> —Professor, University of Minnesota

The American Association of Colleges and Universities stresses in its 2002 report, Greater Expectations: A New Vision for

Learning as a Nation Goes to College, that the current emphasis on "factual recall" is a major barrier to success in college. The report concludes that the students entering college today must be "integrative thinkers who can see connections in seemingly disparate information and draw on a wide range of knowledge to make decisions." Colleges and universities are now focussing on ensuring that their students have a set of strong creative and analytical skills. The report continues to point out that learning is more than the simple acquisition of discrete facts. As students progress through their education, the need for analysis and integration, as well as factual recall, increases. In high school, students need to know facts, but more importantly, they need to be able to know how to interpret and what to do with those facts. Information is transferred into internal knowledge as students begin to apply their understanding to new situations, new problems and new environments. By connecting to their prior knowledge, students develop a deep understanding of the concepts being explored.

Throughout North America, some state and provincial assessments, at various levels, from kindergarten through grade 12, have reinforced a definition of learning as a mere acquisition of unconnected facts. Although efforts have been made at the provincial and national level to make the tests more reflective of the students' ability to apply their understanding, many teachers continue to "teach to the test" with factual knowledge as the basis of instruction. The use of multiple choice tests to monitor student progress, in particular, provides little evidence of a student's analytical skills, resourcefulness, empathy and abilities to apply knowledge and transfer skills from one environment to another, a skill that is needed in post secondary education today.

Conversations between secondary schools and post secondary institutions are not succeeding in defining the skills required for the new learner. There is a misalignment between high school and college entry requirements. It is believed by many that the old lecture model is still the main source of instruction at the post secondary level, and in many cases it is, however, huge changes are coming as a result of the demands of the global economy. The university lecturer is soon to follow the path of the dinosaur, a relic from the past.

"Most colleges do not share with secondary schools what they expect incoming first-year students to know and be able to do to succeed in college. Nor do they make clear to the college bound students why the expected preparation matters."

—Greater Expectations National Panel Report, 2002

In 1956, Benjamin Bloom headed a group of educational psychologists who developed a classification of levels of intellectual behaviour important in learning. Bloom found that 95% of test questions used in schools involved questions that asked students to think at the lowest possible level, that being the recall of information. Bloom identified six levels within the cognitive domain, from the simple recall or recognition of facts, at the lowest level, through increasingly more complex and abstract levels, to the highest order which is classified as evaluation. The categories included the following; knowledge, comprehension, application, analysis, synthesis and evaluation. In 2001, two former students of Bloom, Lorin Anderson and David Krathwohl, published a new version of the taxonomy, based on the research which showed that these intellectual behaviours can be learned and applied simultaneously or out of order. The original taxonomy said that moving from level to level was sequential, you could not apply until you could comprehend, or understanding was required before analysis. It is now believed that these processes can be learned at the same time, or even in reverse order.

A report on mathematical education, funded and released by the U.S. Department of Education, found that core and advanced skills are effectively learned together. The best learning occurred when the students learned basic content and processes, such as rules and procedures, at the same time as they learned how to think and solve problems using those skills. The report also concluded that there is no set age or developmental stage when students are ready to gain complex thinking skills. This is very different than the notion that very young students are concrete and simple thinkers who cannot think abstractly or gain deep understanding of concepts. It is acknowledged that there are basic skills and knowledge that must be acquired, however, these concepts should not be taught in isolation prior to the application of problems solving and critical thinking skills. Learning factual information and the ability to apply, analyse, and solve problems go hand in hand and can be nurtured by using a variety of teaching strategies such as workshops, research projects, dramatization and collaborative learning groups.

> "The common idea that we teach thinking without a solid foundation of knowledge must be abandoned. So must the idea that we can teach knowledge without engaging students in thinking. Knowledge and thinking must be intimately joined."
>
> —Lauren Resnick, Professor of Psychology, University of Pittsburgh

Transfer – Application of Understanding

The process of understanding a concept and being able to apply that knowledge in new situations requires experiences that lead to a transfer of learning. Transfer is defined as the ability to extend what has been learned in one context to new contexts. Teachers hope that students will be able to apply their understanding of a topic from one problem to another within their program and that these concepts will be retained from year to year and applied beyond school. Teachers who focus attention on memorization and rote learning find it difficult to transfer those skills into other areas of the curriculum. Developing understanding through drill and practice focuses solely on remembering by relying on the students' ability to repeat previously taught facts and procedures. Summative testing designed to measure the students' recall of information fails to assess the students' ability to transfer the knowledge and apply it in other situations.

Singley and Anderson, 1989 maintain the importance of practice in developing understanding but emphasize that the kind of practice, in addition to the student's prior knowledge, must also be considered. Many other factors that have important implications for learning must be considered when providing experiences that help promote transfer of understanding. Initial learning of a concept is the first important step in developing transfer. Providing time for students to process new information, combined with effective feedback and "deliberate practice," helps the students internalize their understanding. Creating experiences that are engaging and motivating keep the students' attention on the topic. Integrating the skills and concepts in other areas of the curriculum helps the students make connections and deepens their level of understanding. Finally, having students reflect on what they are learning creates an active relationship between the learner and the concept. Transfer can be improved when the students become aware of themselves as learners and have an understanding of where they are "at" in relationship to the transfer process.

Transfer is deeply affected by the level of initial learning. Without a degree of mastery of the concept, transfer cannot take place. Students cannot apply their understanding when they do not understand what it is they are applying. Formal teaching and deliberate practice of the skill is often required at the early stages of transfer. The use of examples, samples, models and exemplars should be part of the learning experience. Effective use of guided practice where the students are monitored closely as they develop competency, is important for the development of "perfect practice" and understanding.

It is important that teachers give students time to learn complex subject matter. When new concepts are introduced to the learners, they often find it difficult to make connections. They may find the terminology being used hard to process. They may lack an overall understanding of the relevance of the concept. They need time to explore underlying concepts and to create connections to prior learning experiences. The point is that learning cannot be rushed. The process of information processing and integration requires time.

Fish Is Fish (Leo Lionni, 1974)

"Fish is Fish" is a story written for young children but is also relevant for all learners and educators. The story describes a fish who is very interested in learning about what happens on land, but the fish cannot explore land because it can only breathe in water. The fish has a friend, a tadpole, who grows into a frog and eventually goes onto the land. The frog returns to the pond a few weeks later and reports on what he has seen. The frog describes all kinds of things like birds, cows, and people. The book shows pictures of the fish's visual concept of each of these descriptions, each representation is a fish-like form that is slightly adapted to accommodate the frog's descriptions. People are imagined to be fish that walk on their tail fins, birds are fish with wings, cows are fish with udders. This tale illustrates both the creative opportunities and dangers inherent in the fact that people construct new knowledge based on their current knowledge.

New research in the area of cognition provides us with insight about the nature of learning. We now know that students construct knowledge by building on knowledge they have gained previously. Research has also shown that students benefit from working together and the best learning occurs when they teach each other. It is also concluded that student learning increases when exploring real life problems. In short, students learn through making cognitive connections, social connections and experiential connections. All students are unique and therefore each learner makes connections differently. This relatively new information makes it clear that teaching is a complex business and that there is a desperate need for the development of approaches to instruction that are consistent with the research. This new research that shows how the brain processes information has resulted in a paradigm shift at the post secondary level, one from a focus on teaching to a focus on learning. New strategies, such as project-based learning, inquiry-based learning, case-based learning, research-based learning, situation-based learning, action learning and problem-based learning have been incorporated into many classrooms as a way of emphasizing student cognitive development.

Problem-Based Learning (PBL) is an inquiry-based, student-centred educational approach based on current theories of learning. Inquiry is a form of self directed learning that follows four basic stages beginning with the identification of what the students need to learn. In the second stage, resources are identified. Once the learners are aware of the available information, they use the resources and report their learning. The final stage involves the assessment of their learning. PBL is often confused with projects, which are short activities "plugged" into the traditional curriculum. Real Problem-Based Learning, by contrast, is deep, complex and rigorous. The approach had it start in 1960s at McMaster University Medical School as the faculty developed the strategy out of a need to produce graduates who were prepared to deal with the information explosion, and who could think critically and solve complex problems. Soon, medical schools around the world began to adopt the McMaster model.

In these cases PBL is being used as a method that confronts students with problems which provide opportunities for learning. Other educational and professional schools around the globe have modified the model to meet their specific needs.

Many educators and employers have demanded a change in the undergraduate programs at the post-secondary levels, changes that will produce students who can think, solve problems and work in teams. The 1998 Boyer Report, Reinventing Undergraduate Education: A Blueprint for America's Research for Universities recommended the need for these changes and suggested the inquiry-based model as a means for such improvement. The Boyer report does not concern itself with the content of the undergraduate curriculum, but rather recommends ten process-oriented ways that higher education should be changed. They are:

- Make Research-Based Learning the Standard

- Construct an Inquiry-Based Freshman Year

- Build on the Freshman Foundation

- Remove Barriers to Interdisciplinary Education

- Link Communication Skills and Course Work

- Use Information Technology Creatively

- Culminate with a Capstone Experience

- Educate Graduate Students as Apprentice Teachers

- Change Faculty Reward Systems

- Cultivate a Sense of Community

In Problem-Based Learning, students are presented with deep, real-world problems that have been carefully designed to address the course goals and objectives. Students work in teams to solve one or more complex and compelling real world problems. They develop skills in collecting, evaluating and synthesizing resources as they first define and then propose a solution to a multi-faceted problem. Students are asked to summarize and present their solutions in a culminating experience at the conclusion of the activity. The teacher facilitates the learning process by monitoring the progress of each learner and asking questions to move the student forward in the problem-solving process. Unlike the traditional classroom, the teacher is not the "owner" of the information and is not the primary resource. The instructor guides and coaches students as they search out appropriate resources.

Research has shown that Problem-Based Learning provides students with the opportunity to gain theory and content knowledge and comprehension. In addition, the students develop advanced cognitive abilities such as critical thinking, problem-solving and communication skills. PBL can also improve students' attitude towards learning and towards themselves as a learner.

Several studies have been conducted that measure the effectiveness of Problem Based Learning instruction. Overall, most studies show no significant difference in the knowledge acquired by students using the PBL model and the traditional model of instruction. However, it has been found that students who acquire knowledge in the context of solving problems more often apply that knowledge to solve new problems than those students who learned concepts through lectures (Bransford, Franks, Vye, and Sherwood, 1989). Many students participating in Problem Based Learning instruction felt they had developed stronger thinking and problem solving skills as well as more effective communication skills. If our goal as educators is to simply fill the students' bucket with information then the traditional approach to instruction is a very effective model. If we want our students to become engaged in the learning process, to embrace learning and to be able to retain and apply their understanding then new approaches such Inquiry Based or Project Based Learning must be explored.

The Problem-Solving Based Learning Process

There are many way to modify the Problem Based Learning process. There is no one way to teach with PBL and the process is not completely linear. In later chapters, the "Get REEL" approach to learning will be discussed in detail. This model of instruction uses a comprehensive blend of traditional teaching, inquiry based learning and project based learning. Keeping this in mind, I will walk through a basic example of the Problem Based Learning process.

1. Presenting the Problem – There are a variety of ways for a teacher to introduce the problem ranging from reading about it to watching a video or by asking a controversial question. The key is that the introduction must be designed to capture the student's curiosity and interest. Whether through intriguing text or a provocative activity and more importantly the teacher's passion, the goal is always to pull the student into the learning experience.

2. Group Discussion – Following the introduction, the students gather to identify what they already know about the subject and to determine how this prior knowledge may help them solve the problem. They also assess what they need to learn as they discuss possible hypotheses and preliminary solutions.

3. Student Role Assignment – Students may be partnered, grouped or asked to work independently. If groupings are used to solve the problem, members may be assigned roles to assist in the group assignment.

4. Research – Students examine a variety of resources for information which may help them develop a better understanding of the problem. The resources should include text as well as a visual component. This research is usually conducted individually, however, there will be times when group members conduct research together.

5. Group discussion – Following the initial research stage, team members meet to discuss and share what they have discovered. Information is analysed and integrated into the team's understanding of the problem. New hypotheses or solutions may be suggested. It might be decided that additional research is required from their discussions and as a result the research stage might be repeated.

6. Solving the Problem – Students work collaboratively to solve the problem based on the information they have gathered and agreed upon as valid. Students might be asked to submit a written report or share their findings in a class presentation.

7. Culminating Activity – A wrap-up activity, such as a large class discussion, is often used to conclude the activity. This gives the students an opportunity to think critically, apply, evaluate, analyse and synthesize the information.

8. Self and Peer Evaluation – The final stage of the Problem Based Learning process involves reflection on learning and the group experience. This summative reflection on fellow group members' contributions enables the learners to develop the abilities to assess their own performance as well as that of their peers.

No teaching method can be totally effective on its own. Before students can engage in Problem Based Learning, they must have a thorough understanding of the concepts and skills required to explore a problem in depth. It is important that the students have a basic understanding of the core concepts and the related skills that will be used throughout the inquiry process. An understanding of graphs and charts help students as they explore data related information. Effective writing skills are required when students are reporting their understanding of the topic. Knowledge of the stages involved in problem solving or the scientific process are valuable tools for the students to have as they explore a topic. There are times when the teacher must take control of the learning environment and present material using a more traditional model of instruction.

The use of the Problem Based model of instruction has presented teachers with new challenges in assessment. When moving from a process of content mastery of a particular body of knowledge to one of learning to learn, often the traditional methods of evaluation, such as exams, do not work as effectively. New and alternative approaches to assessment must be explored to measure the depth of student understanding, including knowledge, skills, application and attitudes. The use of essays, written reflections, oral presentations, role playing, exhibitions, experiments, self reflection, peer reflection or portfolios can help teachers assess learning by examining the students' actual performance on specific tasks.

As in any effective assessment process, the teacher must begin by fully understanding what they want the students to achieve and how they want the students to get there. It is also important that teachers are aware of the complexity of learning and that it involves knowledge as well as values, attitudes and habits of mind. Assessment of whether goals have been met and learning has occurred should clearly connect knowledge with performance. Has learning gone beyond the facts? Can the students apply their understanding? How to evaluate and assess student learning using the Problem Based Learning model of instruction will be discussed in greater detail in Chapter Six: Assessment Strategies For The 21st Century.

Metacognition

"If the child is going to control and direct his own thinking, in the kind of way we have been considering, he must become conscious of it."

—Donaldson M (1978) *Children's Minds* London: Fontana

"Metacognition" is one of the latest buzz words in educational psychology. It plays an important role in learning to learn. Psychologists such as William James (1890) emphasized the importance of 'introspective observation' but Vygotsky (1962) was one of the first to realise that conscious reflective control and deliberate mastery of cognitive skills were essential factors in school learning. The term was first introduced and published in 1979 by John Flavell. Since then it has become an important concept in the understanding of cognitive development. The term, as defined by Flavell, refers to an individual's awareness of his or her cognitive processes and strategies. It is high order thinking which involves a student's active control of the processes involved in learning. Metacognotion is often simply defined as "thinking about thinking." It is, however, much more complex than that. It is more than different categories such as knowledge of personal variables, task variables and strategy variables (Flavell). Key elements involved in metacognition are:

metamemory – an awareness of which strategies should be used for certain tasks,

metacomprehension – knowing when you don't understand and knowing how to take remedial action to ensure understanding

self-regulation – adjustments made concerning errors.

"Processes of learning and the transfer of learning are central to understanding how people develop important competencies...It is especially important to understand the kinds of learning experiences that lead to transfer, defined as the ability to extend what has been learned in one context to new contexts."

—Bransford, J, Brown, A and Cocking, R (2000). How People Learn: Brain, Mind, Experience and School

Metacognition helps children make the most of their mental resources. It develops as a person gets older and requires an ability to stand back and observe oneself. Asking very young students to be aware of themselves as learners is often a futile exercise due largely to their lack of cognitive experience. Some people are more metacognitive than others when engaging in a cognitive task. Those with greater metacognative abilities tend to be more successful in performances that involve the cognitive process. The good news is that individuals can learn how to better regulate their cognitive activities. Programs such as Cognitive Strategy Instruction (CSI) help students develop thinking skills and processes as a means of enhancing their learning. The main objective of these programs is to enable all students to become more strategic, self-reliant, flexible and productive in their learning experiences.

Metacognitive questioning to raise levels of awareness:

1. Describe what kind of thinking you did.

   What kind of thinking did you do?

   What do you call this kind of thinking?

   Was this kind of thinking...?

2. Describe how you did your thinking.

   How did you do this thinking?

   What did you think about? Why?

   Did you have a plan or strategy?

3. Evaluate your thinking.

   Was your thinking good? Why?

   Did you have a good plan or strategy?

   How could you improve your thinking next time?

Schwartz R. & Parks D.(1994) Infusing the Teaching of Critical and Creative Thinking in Elementary Instruction, Pacific Grove, CA: Critical Thinking Press

While there are many approaches to the instruction of metacognition, the most effective provides the learners with knowledge and or an understanding of the process and allows for experience and practice in using the strategies. Simply providing the learners with the knowledge, without experience, or vice versa, is not enough to develop and sustain metacognitive abilities. Integrating metacognition into the Project-Based model of learning provides an excellent opportunity for the learners to develop their cognitive skills. To be effective learners in the 21st century it is imperative that we give all students the knowledge and opportunity to explore how they learn. If students lack insight into their own learning abilities, they can hardly be expected to self-monitor their growth as independent life-long learners. Knowledge about learning, knowledge about their own learning strengths and weaknesses and knowledge of the demands of the task being explored are critical pieces of information for successful learning. Effective learning combines this understanding with the students' ability to self-regulate through planning, monitoring success and self-correction.

Multiple Intelligences (MI)

In the same way as metacognition has improved under-standing of the learning process, so too, has the growing research on different forms of intelligence. Gardner, in his theory of Multiple Intelligences, proposed the existence of seven relatively independent intelligences: linguistic, logical, musical, spatial, bodily kinesthetics, interpersonal and intrapersonal. In 1997, Gardner added an eighth intelligence, naturalistic. Traditional education over the past century placed a great emphasis on the first two intelligences, linguistic and logical. Gardner's theory has generated a great deal of interest in the educational community. Many educators are seeing the implications of multiple intelli-gences on teaching and learning. New experiential learning programs have been created around this theory. Although the approaches to the development of these intelligences varies widely, the most notable in terms of results, is the modification of traditional curriculum to meet the needs of the learners. The theory of multiple intelligences provides teachers with a number of different approaches to a topic, several ways of having student interact with the concepts and a variety of ways in which students can demonstrate their understanding.

Howard Gardner's Multiple Intelligence Theory was first pub-lished in his book, Frames Of Mind (1983). His theory quickly became established as a classical model by which to understand and teach many aspects of human intelligence, learning styles, personality and behaviour in education.

This simple diagram illustrates Howard Gardner's model of the seven Multiple Intelligences.

Intelligence type	Capability and perception
Linguistic	words and language
Logical-Mathematical	logic and numbers
Musical	music, sound, rhythm
Bodily-Kinesthetic	body movement control
Spatial-Visual	images and space
Interpersonal	other people's feelings
Intrapersonal	self-awareness

"MI theory was not originally designed by Howard Gardner as an educational model to be applied in the classroom. He initially wanted to convince academic psychometricians that there was another, broader way of conceiving intelligence. Ironically, despite arousing controversy, he seems to have failed in this effort. And yet, unexpectedly, he found teachers responding enthusiastically to his model because it filled a need that had not been met by an educational establishment too concerned with standardized measures and lock-step textbook approaches to learning. Instead of treating children as colorless denizens of a bell curve, MI theory revealed the positive qualities of each child and provided practical ways for each child to experience success in the classroom. Thus, the most authentic refutation of the critics of MI can be found in the children themselves. Whenever a light goes on in a child's mind in a well-designed MI classroom, the argument supporting MI theory becomes that much stronger and clearer."

—Thomas Armstrong, Multiple Intelligences in the Classroom

It has been argued, by critics of the MI theory, that it is not research based and therefore has no specific evidence to prove that it has practical applications in the classroom. The problem is that MI is not a program, such as Direct Instruction (Marchand-Martella, Slocum, and Martella, 2003) which involves strict implementation and teacher training. MI represents many techniques, programs, attitudes, tools, strategies, approaches and methods. Teachers are encouraged to use their own special approach to implementing MI with students. It is therefore impractical and impossible to conduct a controlled study on the effectiveness of using MI with learners. Despite the lack of empirical data, there are many other valid sources that prove the effectiveness of MI. Individual studies of student academic improvement, parent reports of improved attitudes towards school, decreased levels of discipline problems, increased performance for students with learning difficulties and documentation of student progress through projects and portfolios, are a few examples of the successful application of MI in the classroom as supported in a study conduct by Kornhaber, Fierro, and Veenema in 2003. The fact remains that MI is being used successfully in classrooms around the world.

Multiple Intelligences is a valuable tool to enhance student learning and engagement, however, there is more involved than simply identifying a learners' intellectual preference. Opportunities must be presented for students to use their strengths and improve their weaknesses. Students need to investigate ideas and concepts by involving their whole selves, including the use of their bodies, imagination, social sensibilities, emotions, as well as verbal and reasoning skills. MI, combined with a positive attitude and a solid academic effort, should lead to improvements in learning.

The Changing Role of the Teacher

The instructors or teachers who use multiple intelligences or inquiry-based learning such as PBL must be willing to give up their role of "sage on the stage" and to assume a new position as "guide on the side", facilitators and learning coaches. For many educators, this can be a challenging and frightening experience, however, it is necessary if students are to reap the benefits of new teaching strategies for the 21st century. Like the students, teachers must be participants in the learning process. The teacher's role is no longer one of dispensing facts and theories. Teachers are now responsible for providing collaborative learning experiences that use continuous formative assessment with great flexibility and attention to meeting the specific needs of each learner. Not only is it possible to achieve such heights, but also incredibly rewarding on many levels, both professionally and personally.

> "In teaching you must simply work your pupil into such a state of interest in what you are going to teach him that every other subject of attention is banished from his mind; then reveal it to him so impressively that he will remember the occasion to his dying day; and finally fill him with devouring curiosity to know what the next steps in connection with the subject are."
>
> —William James, Talks to Teachers, 19th Century

Teachers who inspire students to learn have a clear understanding of what it means to learn. They themselves are enthusiastic learners, who have a deep and current understanding of their subject. They display a love of learning to others and captivate their students through their excitement and passion. Their teaching is student-centred at all times. They are consistently attentive to the welfare of the students and willing to give the time and energy required to meet their needs. These teachers show a clear purpose in their instruction. Their teaching has a direction and momentum. Their standards are demanding and fair as students are encouraged to go beyond their potential.

Effective teaching requires great imagination on a continuous basis. Good teachers should be able to imagine themselves in their students' position and to help their students imagine being in a place of greater understanding than they may be at the time. Having the imagination to anticipate the needs of the students and the imagination to create engaging, relevant and effective ways of presenting subjects is a critical skill for teachers in the 21st century.

Zone of Proximal Development

The Zone of Proximal Development is a term used by Lev Vygotsky (1978) referring to the distance between the learners' actual developmental level and their potential level, the space between who they are and who they are becoming. This space is navigated by the learners under the guidance of informed adults or more capable peers. This "bandwidth of competence" requires assistance and a supportive environment. "**What a child can perform today with assistance she will be able to perform tomorrow independently, thus preparing her for entry into a new and more demanding collaboration.**" Vygotsky saw human growth as a cultural activity that people engaged in together. He was very interested in the role of the social environment and its impact as supports for learning. He defines the social environment as structures for the development of thinking skills that include adults, peers, as well as learning tools (television, books, videos, and technology). The Zone of Proximal Development has led to the creation of new assisted learning programs that emphasize the concept of "communities of learners." The point being made is that learners work effectively in a community environment where they can explore meaning and share ideas together while developing independent learning skills for future use.

The Power of the Question

"A good question in never answered. It is not a bolt to be tightened into place, but a seed to be planted and to bear more seed towards the hope of greening the land-scape of ideas."

—John Ciardi, 1972

In 1912, R. Stevens, in a report entitled "The Question as a Means of Efficiency in Instruction: A Critical Study of Classroom Practice," stated that approximately eighty percent of a teacher's school day was spent posing questions to students. A more recent study, effectively conducted by T. Levin and R. Long in 1981 on teacher questioning behaviours indicated that the pattern has not changed. According to Levin and Long, teachers continue to ask between 300-400 questions each day. The use of questions has been a primary teaching strategy for thousands of years as a means of acquiring factual knowledge and conceptual understanding. Quality, high-level cognitive questions can help facilitate the learning process for students and develop higher order thinking and reasoning skills. Asking good questions should involve an interaction between the teacher and the students. The process of asking the question should never begin and end with the initial question. An ongoing and open dialogue of discovery is created by the open-ended "what if?" question.

In light of the amount of instructional time devoted to asking questions, W. Wilen concludes in his book "Questioning skills for teachers: What research says to the teacher", that most questions asked by teachers involve low- level understanding concerning factual information. Although these types of questions can be used effectively to help improve basic level understanding, low-level questions at the knowledge and comprehension levels (Blooms), do not provide students the opportunity to acquire a deep understanding of the subject matter, nor do they enhance creative and critical thinking skills. There is a need for a good balance of these types of questions if teachers are going to foster student understanding and achievement.

Using good questioning techniques in the classroom can help promote positive student learning, stimulate curiosity, raise self-esteem, increase confidence, enhance student engagement and deepen understanding.

> "Good questions recognize the wide possibilities of thought and are built around varying forms of thinking. Good questions are directed toward learning and evaluating rather than determining what has been learned in a narrow sense."

> —N.M. Sanders, Classroom questions" What kinds" (1996)

Effective questioning techniques can provide the teacher with valuable assessment information needed for improved teaching and learning. When teachers know how students are progressing and where they are experiencing problems, they can use this information to adjust their instructional strategies, such as re-teaching, using a different approach, or offering more opportunities for practice. Good questions should provide quality feedback to both the learner and the teacher. Feedback helps the learners become aware of where they are at in terms of understanding a concept while the teacher provides the guidance and suggestions needed to move to the next step in attaining that knowledge.

While feedback often originates with the teacher, students can also play an important role in assessing their performance through self-evaluation. Students who have a good understanding of the learning objectives and assessment criteria and are given the time to reflect on their work, often show great improvement in their learning. Formative assessment and the power of feedback will be discussed in greater detail in the following chapter.

It is important to create a risk free environment where students can confidently explore imaginative thinking as they make personal connections through predictions, improvising and testing. The process of imagining possibilities begins by the teacher asking questions and generating ideas through open-ended "What if?" or "What if not?" or "How else could this be done?"or "What's the other side of the argument?," questions and scenarios. If we are to develop students who are creative problem solvers, with global awareness combined with empathy for cultural views and who are expected to be life-long learners then the power of the "What if?" question assumes a significant role in 21st century learning.

Chapter Six:
Assessment Strategies for the 21st Century
—Just Give Them The Ball

"Knowledge is not passively received either through the senses or by way of communication; it is actively built up by the cognizing subject."

—Mitchel Resnick

Studies over the last few decades by psychologists and educational researchers have shown that learning is not a simple matter of information transmission. Teachers cannot pour information into the heads of learners nor can knowledge be transferred from a teacher's brain to a student's brain through a series of lectures. Learning is an active process through which people construct new understanding by engaging in active exploration, experimentation, discussion and personal reflection. Simply put, people don't get it, they make it.

Coaching is a very good analogy for effective instruction. Coaching is teaching and one measure of coaching effectiveness is the players' learning, their ability to transfer instructions and drills into performance. Coaching is helping the players improve their skills, through constant observation and feedback, to the point that they no longer think about their actions. The skills become automatic, part of their performance, allowing them the freedom to play the game with confidence. Basketball coaches don't spend large amounts of time giving detailed lectures to their players. Imagine a basketball coach on the first day of practice holding a basketball in his hands and saying: "This ball is orange in colour, 29.5 inches in diameter and weighs 22 ounces. It is inflated to between 7.5 and 8.5 pounds per square inch...." In the minds of every player listening would be the words: "Just give us the ball!"

Basketball is a complex game involving the integration of many skills. Students new to the game begin with the development of simple ball handling skills such as passing, catching, dribbling, making a lay-up and shooting. According to the Fitts' Stage Theory of Motor Learning, students go through three distinct phases when learning a new skill. These sequential and often integrated stages illustrate the process of skill acquisition. The introduction of this new learning occurs during the Cognitive Stage where the learners struggle to make sense of the language involved and find it difficult to translate oral instruction into action. It is difficult for the learners to make a connection to prior learning when the skill is a new experience. The coach makes the learners aware of the need for developing this new skill and shows how it is an important part of the game. At this very early stage of skill development, the learners think, rather than act. Every new move must be carefully orchestrated. The students find it very difficult to differentiate the feel of correct execution and incorrect execution. They show a total lack of body awareness, and as a result require the coach to be their primary source of feedback. During the Cognitive Stage, the skill is often inconsistently performed, usually requiring great effort and determination. For the skill to improve, the learners must concentrate on repetitious practice and receive frequent feedback and modelling to develop consistency. Students who have developed a fear of failure from prior learning experiences often opt out at this early stage of skill development.

The second stage is called the Associative Stage. It is noted that there is not a clear line between these stages because the progression is gradual and individual. As the students execute the action more consistently, they naturally move into this next level. At this point, the skill is performed more consistently although it is still not automatic. To demonstrate the skill, the students must still use full concentration. The learners are beginning to develop an understanding of the difference between correct and incorrect execution of the performance. They are developing a feel or a sense of what is right. Even though they are aware of making a mistake, they are not clear on how to correct it. They must continue to rely on the coach for feedback, but are starting to develop the ability to self-correct and make their own evaluations of their performance. The skill starts to feel more natural and they are able to make sense of the coach's instructions more quickly. It is during this stage that the coach's ability to ask key questions becomes valuable to the learners as they begin to self-correct, while monitoring their own skill development.

> "Repetition, Repetition, Repetition! Practice makes permanent. The goal is to create a correct habit that can be produced instinctively under great pressure."
>
> —Coach John Wooden, UCLA

As performance improves and the skill execution becomes more consistent and requires less conscious thought, the students move to the Autonomous Stage. During this stage, the execution of the skill requires little to no thinking, is consistent and automatic. An internal habit has developed. Once the students reach this stage, thinking is no longer required and can often hurt skill performance. It is hoped that the skill that has been practised, and made a permanent habit, is flawless in its execution. If it has been learned incorrectly, the skill acquisition process must be restarted and full concentration must be committed to making the change.

Assuming the students have developed the skill properly,

thinking interferes in the automatic processing. When performing a lay-up, the body learned the process through repetition, full concentration and specific feedback. To think about the technique would interfere with the body's execution. During this final stage, the learners don't think about doing a lay-up, they just do it. The students' concentration moves from the internal, monitoring the skill execution, to the external, focusing on the basket, while quieting their internal voices to create calm.

"All learning is in the learner, not in the teacher."

—Plato, Greek Philosopher

Learning these basic basketball skills in isolation is of no value unless the students can apply these skills in a game situation. Even though these skills may be mastered by the individual outside game conditions, the speed and complexity of what is happening on the court makes it difficult to display skills under less than ideal conditions. It is one thing to perform a lay-up in practice, it is an entirely different experience when being pressured by an opposing player, while other players jockey for position on the crowded floor. Therefore, coaches design and carefully implement drills that reinforce the skills in a simulated game situation, thus affording the students the opportunity to improve their skills under a variety of conditions. Often these drills and practice activities are used throughout the skill development process while being watched and guided by their coaches. The more opportunities the students are given to rehearse their skills in a guided and simulated situation, the easier it is for them to unconsciously perform during the actual game. The ideal situation is for the students to be able to organize or chunk their skills in such a way as to allow them the freedom to engage in other parts of the game such as play strategies, team work and situational problem solving.

No written word, no spoken plea

Can teach our youth what they should be

Nor all the books on all the shelves

It's what the teachers are themselves

(Author Unknown)

—A favourite poem of John Wooden UCLA Men's Basketball Coach

John Wooden was by definition a great coach. He will always be remembered for his 10 NCAA Championships, a record 88 game win streak and the many great players he produced and coached. When you ask the players he guided, what made him a great coach, they would say that not only did Coach Wooden help make them a great player but he helped make them a great person. Imagine having those words spoken about you as a teacher. That would be powerful.

Two educational psychologists, Ron Gallimore and Ronald Tharp, studied John Wooden during his team practices for a complete season. They recorded each teaching act that Wooden instructed that year. In the book titled, What a Coach Can Teach a Teacher 1975-2004: Reflections and Reanalysis of John Woodens Teaching Practices, they report that of the 2,326 acts of teaching that were observed, only 6.9 percent were compliments. Another 6.6 percent were expressions of concern or displeasure. Over 75 percent of the instructional acts were informative feedback on what to do, how to do it, or when an action needed to be intensified. Wooden used a short three part method to instruct his players; he modelled the right way to do something, showed the incorrect way, and then re-modelled the right way again. His feedback was quick, to the point and specific. John Wooden was a great coach but an even better teacher. When a coach treats the players as students, players and the team often show tremendous improvement. The easiest and most effective way to motivate players is to teach them. All players want to improve their ability to play the game. The coach is responsible for creating opportunities for improvement and to make players aware of their growth by seeing results.

> "...peace of mind that is a direct result of self-satisfaction in knowing you made the effort to become the best that you are capable of becoming."
>
> —John Wooden (Definition of Success)

Assessment For Learning / Formative Assessment

For the most part of the last century, assessment was seen as a way of finding out what a student had learned. It was largely centred on evaluating the effects of instruction. Towards the end of the century, researchers began to look at assessment and evaluation in terms of enhancing student learning, rather than simply measuring it. From this research came a deeper understanding of the evaluation process marking a clear difference between assessment of learning and assessment for learning.

In 1998 Kings College, London, professors Paul Black and Dylan Williams compared the classroom to a "black box". Their studies indicated that many educational and government initiatives focused on the input and output of the box, the box being the student, through the use of summative evaluation while very little attention was placed on what was happening inside the box. They felt that to truly understand what was happening inside the box, there was a need to balance the evaluation process through the use of formative assessment. Formative assessment, which is done during teaching and learning to adapt teaching to meet student needs, stands in contrast to summative assessment. Summative assessment generally takes place after a period of teaching and requires the passing of a judgement about the learning that has occurred, usually by grading a test or paper. Summative diagnostic procedures are assessment of learning, whereas formative evaluation strategies reflect assessment for learning. One focuses on teaching while the other is designed for learning.

> "Assessment for learning is any assessment for which the first priority in its design and practice is to serve the purpose of promoting pupil's learning. It thus differs from assessment designed primarily to serve the purpose of accountability, or of ranking, or of certifying competence. An assessment activity can help learning if it provides information to be used as feedback. By teachers and their pupils, in assessing themselves and each other, to modify teaching and learning activities in which they are engaged."
>
> —Black, P.J. & Wiliam, D. (1998) Inside the Black Box: Raising standards through classroom assessment. King's College, London.

Black and Wiliams define assessment broadly to include all activities teachers and students undertake to gather information, such as teacher observation, classroom discussions, individual conferencing and analysis of student work which may include homework assignments and summative testing. Assessment becomes formative when it is used to adapt teaching to meet the needs of the individual learner and ultimately to raising educational standards. When teachers become aware of how the students are progressing and where they are experiencing difficulties, they can use this information to make adjustments in their teaching by providing a specifically tailored next step for the learners. Instead of looking back on what has been learned, formative assessment helps move the learning process forward by identifying and providing information to help the learners move one step closer to achieving the goal or skill criteria.

Formative assessment might take the form of a teacher giving oral or written comments on how students might improve their performance or it may involve students, assessing for themselves, where their weaknesses lie. The basic assumptions supporting assessment for learning and formative assessment are founded in the belief that all students can learn and can improve their learning and that students need to be actively involved in their own development. Effective assessment strategies should offer the students the opportunity to reflect on what and how they are learning. It is through this reflective process that students experience assessment as part of learning, rather than something separate and removed from learning. Rather than grading a final product, formative assessment supports the steps towards the final product and shows the importance of process in learning. Assessment should answer two very important questions: "How are we doing?" and "How can we do it better?" The "we" is the key word in each question as it implies that learning is a partnership between the student and the teacher.

There are a variety of instructional strategies discussed below, that can be used by teachers to support formative assessment in the classroom. Solid practices used to gather information on student learning, combined with a plan for what will be done with this information, are all part of "good teaching."

Observation is a very basic form of assessment, and when used effectively, can be very beneficial to both the teacher and student. This activity goes beyond walking around the room to see if the students are on task or need help. Through close observation, teachers become aware of both verbal and non-verbal behaviour as they watch the steps the learner is using to complete assignments. The main purpose of observation is to gather information that will help identify where the student is performing and provide the needed data for corrective feedback. When this information is documented, the teacher can monitor the progress of the student over time.

Classroom discussions, with open-ended questions and sharing sessions, create an environment where ideas can be discussed, shared and clarified. These group discussions may involve the teacher and student, teacher and students or students and students. The purpose of this activity is to develop critical and creative thinking skills by giving the students the opportunity to increase the depth of their understanding by sharing understanding.

Written assignments and projects can provide teachers with a deep understanding of how the learners plan, create, organize and develop their ideas. Observing students as they edit and modify their assignments, as well as how they present their understanding, gives some evidence of how the students will perform in the real world. Having the ability to judge and refine their work throughout the learning process is a valuable skill for life-long learners. Classroom assignments provide an opportunity for students to show their proficiency and understanding of the learning objectives. They also provide a means for teachers to diagnose student performance and suggest ways of improving achievement.

Summative assessment involving tests, homework, portfolios and collections of student assignments can be used as formative assessment, if teachers analyse where students are in their learning and provide specific, focused feedback regarding performance and ways to improve. Too often, work is returned to students with a grade or a short comment. Neither is effective for improving student learning. What is required is a clear description of what to do next for improvement.

Extensive research on the effectiveness of formative assessment has been conducted by Black and Wiliams as well as others. The conclusion reached indicates that this form of assessment, with appropriate feedback, produces significant learning gains in test scores when compared to students using a more traditional approach to instruction and evaluation. Research also indicates significant learning gains in low achieving students, providing they become actively involved in the process and use feedback effectively for improvement. (Black and Wiliams, 1998a)

> "...a number of pupils...are content to 'get by'...Every teacher who wants to practice formative assessment must reconstruct the teaching contracts so as to counteract the habits acquired by his pupils."

> —Perrenound, 1991 talking to students in Switzerland

The person who gains the most from formative assessment is the learner, however, for improvement and growth to take place, the student must take responsibility for his/her learning. What is required in the classroom is a attitude of success and a positive mindset that all can achieve. Formative assessment can be a powerful learning tool if it is used and communicated in the right way. While this assessment is effective with all students, it is extremely beneficial for struggling students where it concentrates on specific problems with their work, and gives them both a clear understanding of what is wrong and the achievable steps for getting it right. Students can accept and work with this information, provided that they are not dominated by thoughts about ability, competition, and comparison with others. Those who believe can achieve.

The value of formative assessment is to gain an understanding of what the students know and perhaps do not know. From this information, the teacher makes needed changes in teaching approaches and strategies. The use of specifically designed questions and classroom discussion can be used effectively by the teacher to diagnose progress and ultimately increase the students' knowledge and improve understanding. Asking good quality questions allows for the opportunity for deeper thinking and provides the teacher with significant insight into the depth of students' understanding. Black and Wiliams caution teachers to ask thoughtful, reflective questions rather than simple, factual ones. They also found that the quality of the reflection deepened when students were given adequate time to reply to questions.

> "Formative assessment is essentially feedback to the teacher and the student about present understanding and skill development in order to determine the way forward."
>
> —Harlen and James, Creating a positive impact on assessment in learning, 1996

Feedback given as part of formative assessment helps the learners become aware of where they are in relationship to the desired goal of the learning activity. Effective communication between teacher and students should guide the learners to the next step needed to meet success. The gap that exists between the goal and students' current knowledge or understanding should be defined with specific strategies for improvement. Research conducted by Black and Wiliams and others show that specific and descriptive feedback is an effective and significant instructional strategy to move student forward in the learning process. Descriptive feedback provides the learners with a clear understanding of what they are doing well and what they need to do to reach the next step in their learning. It is not a grade or a "good work" comment but rather specific directions for growth.

Feedback is a critical component for student improvement and begins with the presentation of the learning objectives and criteria for assessment during instruction. Students must understand what they are expected to learn before they can take responsibility for their own learning. In many situations, students do not have a clear conception of what they are learning, why they are learning it and what quality work looks like. In a study conducted by White and Frederikson in 1998, it was found that giving students time to discuss the requirements of quality work and the criteria to be used for assessment, combined with analyzing examples of student work, reduced the achievement gap between low and high achieving students and increased the average performance level of all students in the experimental group. By giving students examples of class tests, student work or assignments, they can see and discuss the difference between good and inferior work. As a result of this process, the students develop an eye for quality that they can use as a standard for their own work.

Research on student self-assessment and self-monitoring, indicates that students who use these skills are more likely to become engaged in their own learning through a feeling of empowerment and a sense of autonomy. A study conducted in 1994 by Fernandes and Fontana indicates that students who are provided with regular opportunities to engage in self-assessment were more apt to see education as an experience over which they had some control. Students could see learning as a result of effort and hard work more than luck, or a result of some unknown variable. When teachers involved students in monitoring their own progress, students were more independent and were able to see how their involvement in learning impacted results on tests and assignments. Self-assessment skills can change the learners from members of a passive audience and move them into the area of active learning.

There are many advantages for using self-assessment as a formative assessment activity. Involving students in the evaluation of their work, and even having them become involved in establishing assessment criteria for an assignment, increases student engagement. By asking students to reflect on their learning, students' interest and attention is enhanced. Self-assessment also provides teachers with information that is not easily measured, such as attitude or how much effort was put into preparing for an assignment. The better the students are at understanding how they learn, the better they will be at discussing their progress with others through discussions or student led conferences.

> "The teacher only knows so much of how much effort you put into it. She has to look over the whole class. You know personally how hard you worked on it and how you worked at home or if you were just goofing off."
>
> —Ross, J. A., Rolheiser, C., & Hogaboam-Gray, A. (1999). Effect of self-evaluation on narrative writing. Assessing Writing

When a grade four student in a classroom that used self-assessment extensively was asked what she compared her work to, she reported, "I usually compare it to my own work because not other people's marks are going on my report card...so I need to see if I improved" (J. Ross, Rolheiser, & Hogaboam-Gray, 2002.) One of the many values of self-evaluation is the focus of a student's attention on explicit criteria, rather than comparisons with other students. Students need to see how they can impact their own learning.

> "The mind aware of itself is a pilot... vastly freer than a passenger mind."
>
> —Marilyn Ferguson

Peer assessment of students by other students aims to improve the quality of learning and empowers learners. It may include student involvement, not only in the judgement made of student work, but also in the establishing of criteria for achievement. Peer assessment and self-assessment are often used in combination as they have many similar advantages. Peer assessment can help improve self-assessment. By placing a judgement on the work of others, students gain an insight into their own performance. Research studies by Brown, Rust, and Gibbs (1994), Zariski

(1996) and others outline the many advantages of peer assessment for students such as increasing motivation through a sense of ownership, creating autonomy, seeing the value of assessment in the learning process, improving self awareness and encouraging deep rather than surface learning.

Teachers will generally need to use summative assessment as a basis for reporting grades or meeting accountability standards, however, the focus of summative assessment for reporting purposes remains quite different from the task of formative assessment to monitor and improve learning. While formal testing shows a snapshot of students at a particular point in time under a test situation, formative assessment allows teachers the opportunity to monitor and guide student performance over time. A comprehensive assessment plan should involve a balance between summative and formative assessment. In so doing, the teacher can establish a clear understanding of where students are in relation to the standards and goals. The more the teacher understands about the student in the learning process, the better he/she can adapt the instruction to meet the needs of the learner.

> "To teach is not to transfer knowledge but to create the possibilities for the production or construction of knowledge."
>
> —Paulo Freire, Brazilian Philosopher and Educational Theorist

Over the past decade, alternative assessment strategies have become a central issue in the debate concerning educational reform. In addition to the more familiar focus upon standardized testing, the discussion has also included the informal, ongoing, formative assessment that occurs within the classrooms. It is how formative assessment is seamlessly integrated into the teaching and learning experience that has generated the most attention.

Assessing 21ˢᵗ Century Skills

The demands being placed on our students as we move forward into the 21ˢᵗ century creates a need for educators to look at new ways to assess student achievement. The global economy requires learners who have a solid understanding of the basics as well as the ability to think critically, to analyse and to make inferences. To help students develop these skills, changes will be needed in the way we evaluate student performance and understanding. Combine this with new developments in our understanding of how students learn and the need for change becomes even more necessary.

> "The notion that learning comes about by accretion of little bits is outmoded learning theory. Current models of learning based on cognitive psychology contend that learners gain understanding when they construct their own cognition maps of interconnections among concepts and facts. Thus, real learning cannot be spoon-fed, one skill at a time."
>
> —Shepard, L.A. (1989). Why we need better assessments. Educational Leadership

Although no one is underestimating the importance of developing basic competency skills, they cannot continue to be the main goal of today's educational system. Many educators are beginning to recognize that minimum basics are not enough and a curriculum is required for matching the skills learned in school to the skills needed when they leave school. It is becoming an expectation that schools develop these skills and competencies in real life, authentic situations, and students are ready to use these "new skills" upon graduation. Assessment strategies are needed that will help students develop these competencies and give teachers the data to measure performance.

Contrary to the understanding of how students learn, many assessments, such as multiple-choice and true and false tests, seldom require the students to apply what they know. These tests fail to show how this learning can be used in the world beyond school. Standardized, summative assessment strategies on their own will not help develop the skills required for the 21st century learners. Alternative assessment strategies that focus on performance and skill development will need to be developed and used to promote the acquisition of these new skills. Strategies that involve asking students to create, perform or produce something, encourage self-reflection and self-assessment, measure outcomes of significance, involve high-level thinking and problem solving skills and invoke real-world applications will become valuable tools for assessment and learning. Performance based assessment strategies, with clearly defined and explicit performance criteria, will help the learners understand what is required of them and will provide teachers with the evidence to modify their instruction on an individual level.

> "Instead of giving the children a task and measuring how well they do or how badly they fail, one can give the children the task and observe how much and what kind of help they need in order to complete the task successfully. In this approach the child is not assessed alone. Rather, the social system of the teacher and child is dynamically assessed to determine how far it has progressed."
>
> —Newman, D., Griffin, P., & Cole, M. (1989). The construction zone: Working for cognitive change in school

James Pellegrino and Naomi Chudowsky, educational testing consultants and University of Illinois professors along with other National Research Council members, developed an assessment triangle (Three Pillars) that consists of, **"a set of beliefs about the kinds of observations that will provide evidence of the students'**

competencies, and an interpretation process for making sense of
the evidence." Pellegrino, in the National Research Council
report, Knowing What Students Know: The Science and Design
of Educational Assessment (2001), define the three pillars on
which every assessment must rest as "a model of how students
represent knowledge and develop competence in the subject
domain, tasks or situations that allow one to observe students'
performance, and an interpretation method for drawing inferences from the performance evidence thus obtained." What this
model illustrates is that quality assessment starts and ends with
defined and meaningful goals for student learning and that the
assessment strategies used must generate information that shows
the depth of understanding and where this understanding is in
terms of the intended learning goals. It is only when the teacher
knows exactly what the steps are to reach the goal and where the
students are in the continuum that true assessment for learning
can take place. This understanding becomes very important for
the development of 21st century skills.

Various nations around the world are working to develop and
define the skills and competencies that will become part of the
21st century curriculum. The International Commission on Education for the 21st Century developed the Four Pillars of Compe-
tency-Based Education as outlined in their UNESCO report
entitled "Learning: the Treasure Within." They define the skills
as: Learning to do (solve daily problems), 2) learning to know
(continuous learning), 3) learning to be (ethically responsible)
and 4) learning to live together (the ability to respect and work
with others). The Partnership for 21st Century Skills defines 21st
century skills as mastery of core subjects along with learning and
innovation skills, information, media and technology skills and
life and career skills. New Zealand in their national curriculum,
Key Competencies in the 21st Century, define key skills as
thinking, using language, symbols, text, managing self, relating to
others and participating and contributing.

It is agreed that these skills, regardless of how they are defined, must be taught to the students. They are not competencies that can be obtained solely through exposure and experience. The intricate elements involved in each skill must be seen as a process. For example, in order for students to successfully understand and apply critical thinking skills, they must first be taught the elements of the process along with the associated jargon. Students begin to develop an understanding of critical thinking when they are given the opportunities to actively engage in experiences and challenging tasks to practice critical thinking. Through the use of "taught" thinking patterns and skills, a shared vocabulary of thinking terminology, consistent and specific feedback on progress and development and encouragement to integrate the skill across the curriculum, students develop a deeper understanding of the skill and its application.

Assessment must be part of a system to support student learning. To successfully achieve this goal, standards and assessment strategies should be clearly outlined and understood by all participants. To do so, the 21st standards and assessments should include the following key elements: 1) specific criteria for each set of skills and a plan that shows the steps required in the development of each skill, 2) performance-based assessment with integration of content knowledge through critical thinking, problem solving and across the curriculum. 3) incorporation of the principles and understanding of learning and cognition, 4) activities and opportunities for thinking to become visible, 5) opportunity for students to display their understanding in ways that are unique to them as learners, 6) the information collected should provide productive and usable feedback for both the teacher and the student.

Assessment of student achievement is changing as a result of the world's demand for new knowledge and abilities. This need combined with research and understanding of the cognitive process, requires teachers to use assessment strategies that effectively show what is happening inside the "black box." Standardized testing cannot be the primary source of evaluating student understanding. Teachers must believe that all students can learn, and in doing so, provide experience for growth and understanding. This can only be accomplished when teachers use methods to fully assess the depth of student learning.

Teaching and learning in the 21st century context involves a deep understanding of how students learn. It is paramount that teachers provide students with opportunities to develop the skills required to be successful in life. There are many challenges ahead for teachers and many educators feel uncomfortable and overwhelmed by the demands being placed on them. There appears to be so much to do, with so many students, and such little time. The expectations of providing learning experiences which challenge learners, while meeting their individual needs, combined with the need for one on one formative assessment to guide learning appears impossible to accomplish. Teachers have to release themselves from the bonds of traditional instruction and embrace new strategies and methods that place students at the centre of their learning. In doing so, teachers will be able to create time for assessing student understanding and providing them with the opportunities to move to the next step in their learning.

Teachers need to explore unique ways to engage and motivate the students as well as giving them the content and skills to become active citizens in the world of tomorrow. To do this requires creativity, commitment, risk and energy. For many teachers, this will involve thinking outside their comfort zone. The changes will involve not only what and how they teach, but also how they measure student understanding and progress. Change is desperately needed and it begins with the classroom teacher. Once the bell rings and the doors are closed, what teachers do is ultimately up to them. The future of our students depends heavily on their understanding of the needs of the "new" world and their initiatives to make a difference.

"Institutions reform slowly, and as we wait depending on 'them' to do the job for us, forgetting that institutions are also us, we merely postpone reform and continue the slow slide into cynicism that characterizes too many teaching careers."

—J. Palmer, The Courage to Teach, 1998

Chapter Seven:
Walking the High Wire: Tools of the Trade

Imagine yourself metres above the raging waters of Niagara Falls as thousands of faces watch and wait for you. Now imagine taking a step forward with only a 10 cm. wide metal wire between you and the waters below. Welcome to the world of the high wire.

High wire walking has a long and interesting past beginning in ancient Egypt and China where rope walkers performed over knives. Since then, many funambulists (aerialists/tightrope-walkers) have performed feats of total amazement ranging from juggling to sword fighting while maintaining balance.

Jean Francois (or Emile) Gravelet, aka Charles Blondin, was considered to be one of the greatest funambulists of all time. He was born in St. Omer, France on Feb. 28, 1824. Blondin became interested in rope walking at the age of five when a travelling circus troupe pitched camp near his home. He came home after the show and immediately strung up a makeshift rope in his back yard between two chairs and started to practice. Blondin's father was a gymnast himself and took the rope-walking interest seriously. He sent Blondin to the Ecole de Gymanse in Lyons that same year. After only six months training, Blondin made his debut as "The Little Wonder". At age 9, Blondin was orphaned and he began performing professionally.

Blondin became obsessed with the idea of crossing Niagara Falls. A year after his initial visit to the falls, he returned to accomplish the feat. The stunt created a great deal of controversy. Many people felt this would trivialize the falls, turning them into a back-drop for a circus act, and should not be allowed. Blondin's original plan was to string his rope to Goat Island, but the owners supported the opposition and denied him permission. Eventually, Blondin was allowed to string his wire a mile further down-stream and on June 30, 1859, he was the first man ever to cross Niagara Falls by tightrope. A large crowd of 100,000 people watched him walk on a single three-inch hemp cord, 1,100 feet long and 160 feet above the Falls at one side and 270 feet at the other.

Blondin made many more trips across the gorge during the next year and became popularly known as "the Prince of Manila" (the rope he used was made of manila.) Each time, he thrilled larger crowds with more exciting acts. He balanced a chair on the rope and stood on it. He took pictures of the crowd while he balanced on the rope. He cooked a meal on a small portable cooker and lowered it to amazed passengers on the Maid of the Mist below. He crossed blindfolded, in a sack, on stilts, and trundling a wheel barrow. On August 17, 1859 he increased the risk by carrying his manager, Harry Colcord, across on his back.

Funambulism is an act involving courage, agility, mental focus, core strength and a deep understanding of the physics of inertia. The survival of the performer depends on his/her knowledge and ability to control balance. If the walker's centre of mass is not directly above the wire, gravity will cause the performer to begin to rotate about the wire. If this imbalance is not corrected, the performer will fall. The walker often carries a long balancing pole. This helps the performer control the rotational inertia, by lowering the centre of gravity and giving time to correct a shift in his/her centre of mass. The use of a balancing and the addition of weights at the end of the pole, provide the performer more time to correct errors.

Now imagine yourself standing in front of a class of thirty students, with only your knowledge of your subject and your understanding of how students learn. You have many tools at your disposal to help maintain your balance. If used effectively, you will create a vibrant learning environment, alive with excitement and energy. If ignored, you and your students run the risk of falling off the wire. Welcome to the world of teaching!

Teaching is a complex business that goes much deeper than simply knowing your curriculum, providing instructional opportunities and testing to see what has been absorbed. The complexity of teaching and learning becomes more apparent as research continues to develop in physiological, cognitive, social and emotional aspects of learning. Teachers need to provide a curriculum that focuses on students mastering the concepts and skills that matter the most in the 21st century as well as giving them the confidence to become life-long learners. Their teaching must engage students and motivate them to want to learn. They need to see the relevancy in what they are learning and see the purpose of their studies.

When moving from a traditional model of instruction towards student-centred teaching, the learners are placed at the centre of the learning stage and the teacher's role is to develop opportunities for engaging the students in experiences that will provide them with a connection to the curriculum. Knowledge of the curriculum and the associated skills and concepts is very important as it forms the foundation for the students to answer critical questions. The essential learning embedded in the courses of study, along with the enduring understandings students are required to assimilate, form the glue that holds the learning model firmly in place. Just as basketball players needs the basic skills to play the game, so too, do students when becoming engaged in the inquiry-based learning process. Teachers must have a firm understanding of how various learning skills can be developed and practised throughout the curriculum. Multiple skills and knowledge areas can be addressed and reinforced through interdisciplinary connections. Often these skills will need to be formally instructed and rehearsed before students can comfortably engage them in the learning process. Once grasped, the skills and concepts need to be seen in terms of the bigger picture. Like the basketball player, it is important for students to see how these basic skills fit into the "game."

A strong understanding of the philosophy and basic elements involved in student-centred learning, inquiry-based, and project-based learning is valuable. Knowledge of the teacher's role in the learning process and the skills required to successfully coach and guide the learners is critical to the development of the students. Teachers should be aware of new research on how students learn, the way cognition is constructed and the process involved in mastering skills. A firm grasp of the fundamentals of formative assessment and an awareness of the power of asking the "right" questions will help teachers move the learners to the next stage in their understanding.

Not all students learn alike, nor can they, nor should they, be expected to show their understanding in same way as others. Learning and developing understanding is personal and complex. The awareness of personal learning styles and preferences, multiple intelligences, personality attributes and so on help the teacher provide valuable experiences that are specifically meaningful for each student.

The Importance of Balance

Balance is as important for schools as it is for the funambulist. It is very difficult to know what has been learned if educators don't balance goals for learning with what is taught, how it is taught and assessed both formatively and summatively. Although research does not provide a guide for creating the "perfect" learning environment, it does support questions about the design of effective learning environments. The degree to which classrooms are student focused, thinking focused, assessment focused and team focused are important considerations for providing a learning culture that motivates, engages and prepares students for the world beyond the walls of the school.

> "... so an individual's knowledge is a function of one's prior experiences, mental structures, and beliefs that are used to interpret objects and events...the mind produces. These models are used to explain, predict or infer phenomena in the real world... much of reality is shared through a process of social negotiation."
>
> —Jonassen, D. H., (1994). Thinking Technology: Toward a Constructivist Design Model. Educational Technology

Student Focused

Students come to school with varying amounts of knowledge. Much of what they have been exposed to both in and out of school forms the basis for further learning. Research suggests that students use their current knowledge to construct new knowledge. What students know and believe internally has a huge affect on how they view new information. A learner's prior knowledge may support the understanding of new concepts or it may be detrimental to learning. Effective teaching begins with understanding what the learners know, their previous knowledge as well as beliefs and cultural practices. Teachers must pay attention to the incomplete understandings and misconceptions about concepts that learners bring with them from prior experiences. They need to build on these ideas in ways that help the students achieve a deeper and more consistent understanding. There is much evidence that learning is improved when teachers pay close attention to the knowledge and beliefs that students bring to a learning situation. Teachers need to use this knowledge base as a starting point for new instruction as they carefully monitor student

progress. For students to modify or change their original understanding, teachers must first help students make their thinking
"visible" so that misconceptions can be corrected. In doing so,
the students can then focus on the next steps required to develop
understanding. This student focused learning environment helps
the students make important connections while providing
teachers with important information for program delivery.

Thinking Focused

Effective learning environments must also be thinking based.
The ability to problem solve using developed thinking strategies
relies heavily on the student's understanding and knowledge of
the basic concepts being explored. This is the point where student
focused environments and learning/thinking environments inter-
connect. Instruction begins with an awareness of the student's
initial preconceptions, attitudes and beliefs about the subject
matter. As illustrated in the Fish is Fish story, learners construct
new knowledge based on their current knowledge. Without being
cognizant of what the students are bringing to the learning experience it becomes very difficult to fully understand what learners
will be able to grasp about the new information. The thinking
based environment encourages the importance of learning to
understand.

A thinking based environment prepares students for flexible
adaptation. Students need to be able to transfer their understanding of concepts to new problems and situations. This is a
critical skill for students who are learning to understand. In
thinking focused environments, the teacher must be aware of several critical features of learning that can affect the learner's ability
to apply what they have learned. Initial learning, student motivation (can they use this knowledge?), the social impact of the
learning (do the students feel they are making a difference?) and

the context in which the learning takes place are important for the development of transfer.

> "Integrating various subjects in the curriculum can contribute to a greater awareness of the interrelationship of school programs and make learning more relevant. Integration of subject content is intended to help students make sense of the many dimensions of their world. Integration also enhances students' ability to transfer the competencies and skills acquired in one context to other appropriate situations."
>
> —The Intermediate Program Policy Grades 4 to 10 December 1993, Province of British Columbia

Presenting students with concepts and skills that are not related or connected creates a situation where understanding becomes disconnected rather than connected knowledge. Integrating the new learning across the curriculum helps students make deeper connections of the relevance of the topic being explored. Integrating the new learning into a theme creates an even deeper level of understanding where the students work with the concepts and skills in a variety of academic situations. With multiple contexts, students are more likely to abstract the relevant features of the concepts while seeing the degree to which various subjects share common elements.

> "Students develop flexible understanding of when, where, why, and how to use their knowledge to solve new problems if they learn how to extract underlying principles and themes from their learning exercises. [But] many assessments measure only propositional (factual) knowledge and never ask whether students know when, where, and why to use that knowledge."
>
> —J. Bransford, A. Brown, and R. Cocking, How People Learn: Brain, Mind, Experience, and School

A school environment that provides opportunity for transferring knowledge from school to everyday environments should be the goal of every school program. Making the learning relevant and aligned with the real world are important considerations. It is also important to help learners choose, adapt and invent strategies for solving problems. Creating experiences that enable students to explain, extend and explore while seeing the importance of the topic helps students make sense of what they are learning. Creativity, critical thinking and independence are valuable skills for the 21st century learner and a prerequisite for the life-long learner. In order to develop these skills, students need to have a firm understanding of how they learn and to be able to reflect on their own thinking. Metacognition increases students' abilities to connect learning by helping them gain an understanding of how they acquire content knowledge. In the thinking environment, teachers help students develop the ability to monitor and regulate their own understanding and thinking in such a way that they become independent thinkers who can self-monitor, self-assess and self-regulate.

Assessment Focused

> "A score, by itself, is the least useful form of feedback; rubrics provide a great deal more and specific comments in reference to the rubrics—contextual feedback—provide still more."
>
> —Grant Wiggins, Educative Assessment

In addition to being student focused and thinking focused, an effective learning environment must also be assessment focused. Learning to understand requires consistent use of formative assessment and feedback. Understanding and transferring new knowledge should focus on understanding and not only on memorizing procedures and facts, although these skills can be of value to the learner. Opportunity for feedback must be continuous, consistent and part of the program delivery. Feedback is intended to assist the students by making their thinking "visible" and helping them move forward one step at a time in developing their confidence and competence. It should be constructive and not intrusive, providing students opportunities to revise and enhance the quality of their thinking and understanding. An effective assessment learning environment also encourages students to build skills of self-assessment. In this environment, students learn to assess their own work as well as that of their peers in order to help everyone learn more effectively.

Effective learning environments that focus on the learners, include the use of portfolios, a format of keeping records of students' work as they progress throughout the year. Portfolios allow students to demonstrate their achievements with their teachers, peers and parents. When used effectively, they provide the learners and others with valuable information about learning for understand, personal growth and metacognition.

Team focused

Successful learning environments that are student and thinking centred and assessment focused require the cultivation of a culture that promotes a sense of community. "We" are a team and "we" are in this together. The team focused learning environment works on several levels; the classroom as a learning community, the school as a community of learners and the connection of the students to the world beyond the school through the creation of partnerships in their community.

The creation of a classroom as a learning community is based on the development of a culture of acceptance. Students need to feel safe, physically and emotionally. They need to know that the norms established in the classroom by teacher and students reflect fairness, inclusion and a sense of caring combined with expectations that value learning with rigour and high standards. An environment, that shares these norms, increases opportunities for students to interact, collaborate, share ideas, solve problems, receive feedback and learn.

The school as a community of learners is largely affected by the adults who work in the building. The relationship among staff members, students and students, and students and staff, set the tone for the learning environment. The philosophy and beliefs of the teachers are critical to creating a team atmosphere, one that is supportive and encourages excellence and commitment. Seeing each member of the school community as a "learner" is important in creating an environment of respect and trust. Education is a life-long process that involves everyone, staff and students alike. Education is a business of learning and growing.

Connections beyond the walls of the school to the broader community are vital for creating and maintaining an authentic learning environment. Learning does not just happen at school. When one examines the amount of time a student spends in school compared to other settings such as home, community centres, part time work, and so on, it becomes apparent that what happens outside school has a huge impact on students' academic achievement. Establishing powerful learning partnerships within the community can expose students to relevant and engaging information from professionals in the field. Connecting and collaborating with out-of-school contacts provides valuable learning experiences for both the students and the teachers by providing a window of reality and creating a 'feel' for what happens in the "real world." Transfer of learning takes on a new light when students see the immediate application of what they are learning and how it applies to the outside world.

"From the standpoint of the child, the great waste in school comes from his inability to utilize the experience he gets outside....while on the other hand, he is unable to apply in daily life what he is learning in school. That is the isolation of the school... its isolation from life."

—John Dewey (1916)

Designing a successful learning environment requires alignment among the four perspectives: student focused, thinking focused, assessment focused and team focused. Each has the potential to overlap and influence the other. Attention should be placed on making each a vital part of the learning experience. Effective teaching is like walking the high wire. Control over the forces of nature requires attention to the tools that can help maintain a strong centre of gravity and ensure balance.

The Delivery Process

It is important that teachers have a clear understanding of how the learning experience can be translated into action. A strategic plan or model should be created that is used for program delivery. The model used in the Get REEL model is based on the APAA (Awareness, Passion, Audience, Action) model. The first stage of the model involves the development of key skills that will be used throughout the program. Along with these skills, the students are provided with opportunities to explore the magnitude and depth of the problem thus forming a basic understanding upon which further connections are made. As the students continue to develop a deeper understanding of the topic, they are encouraged and guided to find an area of genuine and unique interest in a particular aspect of the problem. By exploring an interest in depth, that is valued by them personally, students begin to form a passion for the topic. Students are then given choices of how they will display their understanding to an audience of their peers. In the final stage, students are encouraged to move their passion beyond the curriculum in a form of action.

APAA – A Plan of Delivery

Awareness

Awareness is a person's ability to perceive, to feel or to be conscious of what is around them, such as events, experiences or objects. Human survival is heavily dependent upon their ability to be aware of something. The development of the human brain and its capacity to learn has been an evolutionary process involving adaptation and survival. The adaptive behaviour of humans is dependent on their ability to be cognizant of their environment and their ability to respond to a situation. The adaptive decision is based on the individual being able to compare, categorize, organize, analyze, integrate and evaluate the information. When processing information, the brain consciously focuses on external stimuli, and at the same time, processes the information on a subconscious level where connections and relevance are assessed. The individual's capacity to learn depends deeply on how that information is processed on the subconscious level of awareness.

The function of the teacher is to facilitate learning by helping the students focus their awareness and attention on the information being introduced. The most effective way to accomplish this is to teach to the brain's natural capacity for making associations. "Every complex event embeds information in the brain and links what is being learned to the rest of the learner's current experiences, past knowledge, and future behaviour." (Caine and Caine, Making Connections: Learning the Human Brain) A focus on making students aware of and alert to the new experience is required for the brain to become interested. The learner's internal instinct to make connections and to seek meaning of the experience must be triggered, resulting in a state of curiosity and attention.

Students have many preconceptions and prior experiences with many of the areas of studies in school. Their prior learning, biases, conceptions, and misconceptions are all stored in their long term memory. At the awareness level, the teacher needs to focus on the students' prior understanding and connections to the topic being explored. They must make the students "knowledge" visible by moving it from long term memory into working memory, the part of the brain where adjustments, modifications and new learning takes place. Learning is optimized when the students see how the new learning builds on prior learning.

The introduction of new concepts is a critical stage in the learning process. How the information is delivered is a crucial factor for ensuring student engagement. There has to be a "personal" reason or connection for the students to view the information as worth learning. The relevancy and usefulness of the new information is a consideration of importance to the learners. Students need to see how the new concepts connect to and build on their prior learning and how they can be used for future understanding. The way this knowledge connects to the realities of their world beyond school is important and answers the question, "Why do we need to know this?"

Topics and concepts, that establish the relevancy on an "it matter to us" basis, demand more attention from the learners. When students can see the "local" significance of what they are studying they tend to place a greater level of commitment on the need to understand. Because they see the significance of the learning on a personal level, it takes on a deeper need for awareness. The concept of global warming is a deep and complex topic that many students feel happens somewhere else in the world.

Only when the affects of global warming are introduced at the local level, with impacts that affect the students personally, do they see the need to sit up and pay attention.

Learners process information using both sides of their brain hemispheres, although one side is usually more developed, thus making some subjects easier to learn than others. Most students have a primary preference for learning material involving the use of their senses. The VAK (Visual, Auditory, Kinesthetic) learning styles model describes how the senses are used. Visual learners are those who tend to learn and recall information best when it is presented visually. Auditory learners learn best by hearing the information and kinesthetic learners are those who learn best by touching or manipulating information. Students often use a combination of all learning styles when working with new experiences. Effective teachers are aware of the learning styles of their students and incorporate the three styles into each lesson.

A great example of how one teacher uses visual, auditory, and kinesthetic techniques depending on his/her students' styles is found in Hollywood. Robert Easton is known as the Dialect Doctor and Mr. Fix-it of Phonemes. He has cured accents and strengthened dialects for thousands of actors, including Bruce Willis, Denzel Washington, Natasha Richardson, Al Pacino, Jane Fonda and Tom Hanks. He states that people learn in three different ways.

> "Some are very "ear-minded," or auditory. They can hear something and repeat it with almost tape-recorded fidelity. Robin Williams is a great example of that. For his role in Good Will Hunting, we worked on perfecting a very subtle Boston accent. All we did was to sit together and talk. He has a phenomenal ear. Others rely on their visual competence. Charlton Heston is a wonderful example of what I call "eye mindedness." He would send me his scripts, and I'd respell his dialogue

for him in a visual transliteration that we had agreed on-what we call "Easton's Half-Assed Respelling." He learned by seeing. And some people I teach kinesthetically: I tell them exactly what to do with their mouths, when to vibrate their vocal chords and how to move their jaws to produce a particular sound."

—Robert Easton, Hollywood Dialect Doctor

Too often, students are required to learn material in ways that are in conflict with their learning styles. To capture and maintain a students' interest in a topic and to create a desire for them to become actively engaged requires a carefully orchestrated lesson delivery involving multi-modal learning. This can be achieved by using a variety of resources and providing opportunities for sharing and discussing information. For the learners to make connections to prior learning, they need to establish a basic understanding of the overall concept and how it will be of value to them.

The development of an overall awareness of the topic being explored lays the foundation for engagement and understanding. The more a teacher can "front load" information, the better the chances are for connection and transfer of learning to take place. Student abilities and competencies are varied in every classroom. Some students have a deep connection to the concept being explored while others have little to no prior learning to build on. The teacher must find ways that help "pave the road" for each learner to meet success. For example, reluctant readers may need to see the concept visually in the form of a video or hear it musically. Learners, regardless of their strengths and weakness, deserve the opportunity to be part of the learning "game". This can only be accomplished when we engaged them through the process of awareness and do it in ways that address the learners' personal style of making connections.

Passion

Competence in a concept is developed through deep understanding and engagement. Students learn more when the concepts are personally meaningful to them. In order to have a deep understanding of a topic, students not only need to know relevant facts, theories and applications, they must also make sense of the topic through the organization of those ideas into a system of understanding. The development of this system requires that the students learn concepts and skills in ways that are relevant and meaningful to them. The learning has to be personal and authentic, involving deep understanding and a sense of purpose for future use or in the production of something meaningful such as a presentation or project.

Providing students with the opportunity to become "experts" in an area of special interest, gives them a reason to become engaged and can lead to a deeper passion for the topic. Empowering the students with the opportunity to explore, discover, discuss, share and present their "special" understanding creates learning that engages their minds and hearts. Allowing students the freedom to explore their passions, while connecting their interests to the new learning being introduced, can be powerful and can lead to deep involvement and understanding.

Audience

"Teaching is the highest form of understanding."

—Aristotle

The best way for students to show comprehension of a concept is for them to teach it to someone else. Teaching calls for complete understanding of the material. It is not a matter of "kind of getting it" or knowing enough to pass the test. Teaching requires deep and thorough understanding. Teaching forces the students to communicate their thoughts clearly and precisely. The new global economy has created a society that is becoming interlocked and interconnected, resulting in a need for cooperation and collaboration among its citizens. This cooperation requires effective communication skills where being heard is not enough. What is even more important is that you are understood. The power of the "story teller," as described by Daniel Pink in his book, A Whole New Mind, will depend greatly on the ability to be articulate and persuasive. Peoples' ideas will be only be effective when they have the ability to make others comprehend what is being said. Teaching helps the learners develop important skills of describing ideas well enough for other students to understand. These valuable skills can only be experienced by providing the students with an audience.

Mimi Wagner and Ann Gansemer-Topf in their article Learning by Teaching Others: A Qualitative Study Exploring the Benefits of Peer Teaching, shows the value of peer-to-peer teaching and how it can enhance student learning. The integration of peer teaching and learning-by-doing into a course of study proved to be a valuable and effective learning tool. Students involved in the study reported that the peer teaching experience increased their understanding of the subject matter and improved their ability to apply concepts in new settings. They found themselves encouraged to take initiative and responsibility for their own learning.

Action

A class of grade eight students in Lansdowne, Ontario is playing an active role in the fight to save a wetland in their neighbourhood. Wetlands play a crucial role in helping to minimize the erosion of land, and the wetland in Lansdowne is also home to a diverse range of waterfowl, amphibians and other animals. Students at a local public school became involved after they learned that the wetland near their school had become a dumping ground and a home to litter and waste. As part of their study of water systems, the students decided to plan a community action project to bring awareness about the importance of the wetland. The students wanted to make a change and got involved in hosting a clean-up day.

Students want to make a difference. They have a need to become involved in doing things that have an impact on others. There are many out-of-school organizations such as iEARN (International Education and Resource Network) the world's largest non-profit global network, which enables teachers and youth to use the Internet and other technologies to collaborate on projects that enhance learning and make a difference in the world. Many students, when exploring their particular passion for a topic, find a need to take their excitement to the next level where an action is required. It is at this point where learning takes on energy of its own. The true application of the learning experience moves beyond the classroom and spills over into the community, creating a ripple effect felt by all. The learners become empowered and inspired and they seek every opportunity to engage others in their excitement. This is the ultimate stage of learning.

Chapter Eight:
Get REEL – Bringing It All Together

"The true 21st century learning revolution is that learning
– training and schooling – is finally throwing off the
shackles of pain and suffering which have accompanied
it for so long. Within most of our lifetimes pretty much
all learning will become truly learner-centred and fun –
fun for students, fun for trainers and teachers, fun for
parents, supervisors administrators and executives. The
huge wall which has separated learning and fun, work
and play for the last few hundred years is finally beginning to tremble and will soon come tumbling down, to
everyone's benefit. And while it will continue to resist
for a while yet, like the Berlin Wall in the political world
when it finally falls there will be a stampede to
freedom."

—Marc Prensky, Digital Game Based Learning

Get Reel -Relevant, Engaging, Enduring, Learning

As our students move forward into the 21st century, they will
need to be prepared to meet the challenges of the new global
community. The world is changing at a rapid pace and with this
change comes the need for opportunities to develop "new" skills.
Students must move beyond basic competencies in core subject
areas. To be effective members of the world of work and to contribute as productive members of their communities, students

will be required to develop skills that will allow them to actively compete in a highly competitive world market that has expanded beyond boundaries. Critical thinking and problem solving skills will be critical for all students as they approach new challenges and opportunities. Effective collaboration and communication skills will be important as the students engage in a world of local and global networking, selling ideas, creating designs, displaying empathy, carefully crafting stories. New technologies and work strategies will require agility and adaptability as students find themselves in turbulent, and often, uncharted waters. Being capable of accessing, analysing and seeing the significance of information and data will be increasingly important as the information explosion expands.

The same skills that will give the students a competitive advantage in the world of work, will also provide them with the requirements to be good citizens. The people of the world must face many difficult challenges and solve serious problems. With new technological advancements come serious environmental, ethical and moral questions that must be addressed.

Today's learners must be prepared to meet the many challenges of the 21st century. They need to be given the opportunity to develop 21st century "life" skills. Get REEL is an instructional approach designed to introduce these skills in a relevant and engaging way. Get REEL challenges the students to make wise informed decisions through an "experiential" approach to learning. This cross-curricular model of instruction blends traditional teaching, critical thinking, inquiry based learning and project based learning.

Theoretical Basis to the Get REEL Approach

Constructivism

There are many different views on "constructivism", however, a common characteristic lies in the understanding that learning is an active process rather than passive. The history of constructivism in education and philosophy has been around for many years dating back into the 18th century with the works of Vico and Rousseau and continuing into 20th century with John Dewey. Dewey argued that "education is not a preparation for life, it is life itself."

> "Cognition theory concentrates on the conceptualization of students' learning processes. It focuses on the exploration of the way information is received, organized, retained and used in the brain."
>
> —Thompson, A. D., Simonsen, M.R., Hargrave, C. P. (1996). Educational Technology A Review of the Research

A major goal for constructivism in education is the creation of a rich learning environment where emphasis is placed on the uniqueness of the learners and the provision of a specialized experience to meet those individual differences. B.G. Wilson in his book, Constructivist Learning Environments: Case Studies in Instructional Design (1996),defines a constructivist learning environment as "a place where learners may work together and support each other as they use a variety of tools and information resources in their guided pursuit of learning goals and problem solving activities."

Experiential Education

> "Every living creature, while it is awake, is in constant interaction with its surroundings. It is engaged in a process of give and take, of doing something to objects around it and receiving back something from them, impressions, stimuli. This process of interaction constitutes the framework of experience."
>
> —John Dewey, How We Think: A Restatement of the Relation of Reflective Thinking to the Educative Process, (1933)

The term experiential learning has come to mean "learning by doing." A learning experience is said to be experiential when the students take an active role in the experience and uses reflection as a way of processing and understanding the concepts. The goal is to develop knowledge and skills through direct involvement and real world examples. The concept of integrating experience into the learning process has a strong historical background. In 1787, Immanuel Kant, a German philosopher argued that both rationality and experience gave order to the construction of knowledge. John Dewey, in his book Experience and Education (1938) believed that "educative" experiences were valuable in developing intellectual and moral growth. Dewey also saw traditional education as hierarchical and undemocratic and that good citizenship required student participation in aspects of the school program. Kurt Hahn, a great 20th century educator, saw school experience as a means to developing social responsibility.

The pervasiveness of experiential education makes learning exciting, absorbing and compelling for the students. Experiential learning is supported by the principle of holistic education, a process that blends cognitive development of understanding with emotional development for maturity. Education for knowledge and maturity is based on "optimal learning", which involves not only cognitive learning but also affective learning or emotional intelligence. The learner's emotions provide the meanings which are essential to learning.

The most obvious indicator of experiential education is the role played by both teacher and learner. The teacher becomes a facilitator of the learning experience while the student becomes actively involved while assuming additional responsibilities and ownership over the process of learning. Every effort is made to connect learning to real life experiences, while giving the learner the opportunity to think critically and apply understanding of new concepts and skills in novel situations.

Integrated Curriculum

There are many definitions of an integrated curriculum. A basic definition is presented by Humphrey et al (Humphrey, Post, and Ellis, Interdisciplinary Methods: A Thematic Approach, 1981) when he states, "An integrated study is one in which children broadly explore knowledge in various subjects related to certain aspects of their environment." Other descriptions go further to define this approach as learning and teaching in a holistic way, with direct reflection and interaction with real world issues (Shoemaker, Integrative Education: A Curriculum For The Twenty First Century, 1989). The Dictionary of Education defines interdisciplinary curriculum as "a curriculum organization which cuts across subject-matter lines to focus on comprehensive life problems or broad based areas of study that bring together the various segments of the curriculum into meaningful association" (Good, Dictionary of Education, 1973). Jacobs, expands the definition by claiming that integrated curriculum is a "knowledge view and curricular approach that consciously applies methodology and language from more than one discipline to examine a central theme, issue, problem, topic or experience" (Jacobs, Interdisciplinary Curriculum: Design and Implementation, 1989).

- an integration of subjects or concepts within a subject area
- the use of projects
- resources that go beyond the textbook
- exploration of relationships among concepts
- use of Thematic units for organization
- flexible schedules
- flexible groupings
- assessment for learning

An integrated curriculum is characterised as: interwoven, connected, thematic, multidisciplinary, correlated, linked and holistic. Its primary purpose is to maximise and enhance learning, both within and across learning areas of the curriculum. This approach to learning reflects real-world experiences more accurately and better fits a newer understanding of how students learn best.

Living in the world beyond the walls of the school involves a deep understanding of integration. Most jobs require the knowledge and application of a wide range of skills. Often, workers are presented with problems and asked to solve them. They may be given some guidance, but seldom receive direct instruction. The success of the employees is based on their ability to solve the problem, individually or as members of teams. A school system that gives students a set of isolated facts and asks them to memorize and recite them, without the opportunity to apply understanding, does not prepare the learners for life outside school. Disconnected information can often lead to apathy, while integration can lead to connections.

There is a need for teachers to restructure their thinking and to consider using an integrated curriculum approach in their teaching. The integrated curriculum's energy is generated by the benefits to students and teachers, through their learning experiences. Holistic in principle, integrated teaching means that students get to see the big picture, instead of fragments. This allows them to connect what they learn in school, to their own life experiences, and across subject areas. Curriculum integration is a way of making education more meaningful.

In addition to the understanding that an integrated curriculum helps make learning manageable and relevant, it also provides a learning experience that is consistent with current research about how the brain processes and organizes information. The brain organizes new information by connecting to previous experiences. The human brain effectively processes many things at the same time and holistic experiences are recalled, quickly and easily by the learner. Shoemaker (Integrative Education: A Curriculum For The Twenty First Century) writes "The human brain actively seeks patterns and searches for meaning through these patterns." This research is further supported by Caine and Caine (1991) when they discuss the connections between neuro-psychology and educational teaching strategies. They believe that searching for meaning and patterns is a basic process in the brain. In fact, they go even further to suggest the brain might resist fragmented facts that are presented in isolation. Caine and Caine, as well as Shoemaker, argue that learning occurs more quickly and thoroughly when it is presented within a meaningful context, with an experiential component. While the brain's holistic approach to learning is universal, it is also recognized that learners are unique in terms of their learning styles. To meet the unique nature of the learners, teachers must provide students with choices of how they will develop their understanding and how they will display what they know.

The climate of an integrated classroom is less regulated, more flexible and interactive for both the teacher and students. Modes of teaching are often group based. Within groups, students share their personal knowledge and experiences, further building onto what they know and will learn. The teacher is available to guide research, provide relevant material and /or assist the learners and simultaneously assess progress.

The Power of the Integrated Theme

Inquiry-based learning, along with project-based learning, case-study learning and problem-based learning are all strategies that are used in the processing of information. Students are engaged in activities that help them actively ask questions, research information, think critically, solve problems and draw conclusions about issues of importance to them and to the world around them. Students are presented with an issue or theme that is often current, controversial and relevant to them and their community. Curriculum connections are carefully woven through the fabric of the study providing the learner with content and information that is critical to the understanding of the topic being examined. As students become independent explorers, they develop a plan of study that will involve them as researchers, writers, technologists, computer programmers, play-writes, interviewers, debaters, actors and activists. The students see themselves doing valuable work on issues that address essential questions and important standards. The students' excitement and passion for making a difference becomes the driving force behind their study. The teacher's passion and deep understanding of the many learning processes involved and on-going feedback gauges the journey to a desired outcome.

Because inquiry-based learning is driven by the students and monitored by the teacher as a facilitator, it is often believed that this approach to student learning is unstructured and capable of getting out of control. Inquiry-based learning is not unstructured but simply structured differently than traditional methods. Successful implementation of this strategy depends deeply on teacher planning, classroom management, preparation and responsiveness. Much of the organization and planning is done up front allowing the teacher the freedom to move into the role of learning coach.

Karen Sheingold, in her book Keeping Children's Knowledge Alive Through Inquiry, (1987) explains what makes the inquiry process effective. Sheingold argues that the success of this approach is based on the students': opportunity to build on their existing knowledge, working with topics of interest to them, exploring and using a variety of resources, using technology as a tool for learning, being given the opportunity to show their understanding in ways that are unique to them, sharing and communicating with real audiences, evaluating their progression in both process and product and evaluating themselves, their peers and the value of their resources.

> "Who questions much, shall learn much, and retain much."
>
> —Francis Bacon, philosopher, statesman, essayist

The advantages of using inquiry-based learning strategies go beyond giving students the opportunity to becoming engaged in the learning process while developing problem-solving skills. Students who have struggled in the traditional classroom where lectures, memorization and tests define their failures, often grow in confidence and self-esteem when given the freedom to explore their own learning. In addition, inquiry-based learning is designed in such a way as to allow for cross-curricular integration of subjects, content and skills under the same issue of study. It is also well suited for the development of team building skills as well as collaboration and cultural understanding. Although students do not always have to work with partners or in teams, an environment needs to be established to reinforce those particular skills.

Backward Design

The use of theme based units of study is a vehicle through which a range of curriculum concepts can be successfully integrated into the learning environment. This method of teaching connects curriculum strands and builds on the students' interests and life experiences, while creating a sense of purpose and community in the classroom. Having students explore a theme that is important and relevant to them creates a culture of inquiry and communication and a commitment to learning that is meaningful and worthy of their time and attention.

The thematic, integrated study approach, requires a deep understanding of curriculum content and detailed, up front planning. The role of the teacher becomes one of facilitator or coordinator who must maintain a sense of direction and an understanding of how the concepts being explored and the skills being developed connect to enduring understandings. Enduring understandings go beyond facts and skills to focus on concepts, principles and processes that are part of the bigger picture.

The planning process is critical to the success of the thematic, integrated model. The teacher is the designer of the student learning and must be able to clearly identify the learning goals, blend assessment strategies that will assist student understanding and create effective and engaging learning experiences. Understanding by Design (UBD) is a framework created by Grant Wiggins and Jay McTighe and is a valuable tool for the development and implementation of integrated studies. UBD is based on the principle that the goals of education should be to develop and deepen understanding by providing opportunities for learners to explain, interpret, apply, shift perspectives, empathize and self-assess. These elements of understanding can help teachers identify the enduring understandings that students will think deeply about throughout the unit and provide a template for how students will show their understanding. They are identified as being able to:

explain: provide thorough, supportable and justifiable accounts of phenomena, facts and data interpret: tell meaningful stories; offer apt translations; provide a revealing historical or personal dimension to ideas and events

can apply: effectively use and adapt what we know in diverse contexts

have perspective: see and hear points of view through critical eyes and ears; see the big picture

can empathize: find value in what others might find odd, alien, or implausible; perceive sensitively on the basis of prior direct experience

have self-knowledge: perceive the personal style, prejudices, projections, and habits of mind that both shape and impede our own understanding; aware of what we do not understand and why understanding is so hard.

Wiggins and McTighe state in their Understanding by Design model, that curriculum development is a three stage design process called "backward design." The design process begins with the end in mind or the learning goals and essential understanding of what the teacher wants the students to acquire at the completion of the unit. The Understanding by Design process is driven by three stages, each with a focussing question:

Stage 1 – What is worthy and requiring of understanding? (Essential Understanding/Enduring Learning)

Stage 2 – What is the evidence of understanding? (Assessment Strategies)

Stage 3 – What learning experiences and teaching promote understanding, interest and excellence? (Learning Experiences)

The framework begins with what the students need to know, moves to what that learning will look like and finishes with selecting learning experiences and opportunities for students to develop a deep understanding. The learning experiences provided should require the students to:

> "...theorize, interpret, use or see in perspective what they are asked to learn...or they will not likely understand it or grasp that their job is more than recall."
>
> —Wiggins and McTighe, Understanding by Design.

Selecting the Theme for Integrated Project Learning

Selecting an appropriate theme or topic for an integrated project-based unit requires many considerations. The topic must be real, relevant to the learners, controversial and capable of being integrated into many areas of the curriculum. The selected topic should provide teachers and learners with the opportunity to cover the essential learning and enduring understandings required by the curriculum in addition to offering experiences for collaboration, critical thinking and problem solving. The theme should allow for a balance between formal instruction of content and skills as well as give the students the freedom to inquire, question, experiment and express their own thoughts, ideas and opinions. Topics such as the environment, global warming, social injustice, world economy, global conflict and media and technology are some of the many areas that allow students to become engaged at a local and global level. Often these topics are current and information is easily attainable. Students need to be able to explore a variety of information sources including text, guest speakers, magazines, websites and video, as they develop their foundation of understanding. The wider the information sources, the deeper the students become engaged in the learning experience. All students need to be given the opportunity to become involved in the topic regardless of their learning strengths.

Young people like to argue. Controversy is part of their world and many students are masters of the debate, although they often lack the tact and formal skills involved. Playing the devil's advocate comes naturally to them. Selecting a topic that has a variety of view-points can be very exciting for the learners. Allowing them to explore a topic from a different vantage point creates an understanding of acceptance. Students want opportunities to express and share their opinions with others. Opinion writing, debates, trials, simulations, role playing, blogging and discussions are some of the many experiences effective teachers can use to engage their students.

The Essential Question(s)

Once a topic has been selected, it is important to create relevance at the community level. The importance of the topic must be felt locally. The students need to see the impact the learning experience will have on their own lives and how those around them will be affected. Bringing the experience to the heart of the students creates a demand for attention and a focus on a need for understanding. For this reason, each topic or theme should be driven by one, or more essential questions. Everything that is taught, explored and discovered is reflected back to the essential question. Global warming, for example, is an issue that is being felt world-wide, however many students fail to see the local significance. Students living around the Great Lakes or along the St. Lawrence Seaway, for example, should understand the impact global warming has on their waterways and how this will affect their communities on many levels. Creating an essential question that reflects this local concern is a valuable tool for creating engagement and helping the students form connections for learning. The more opportunities a student is provided to become connected to the topic, the greater the awareness, the better the chances are for developing a passion and the stronger the need for action. Students want to make a difference and it is the responsibility of teachers to help the learners become informed and prepared to make an impact.

Enduring Understanding/Essential Learning (Skills Required)

Integrating concepts across the curriculum allows students to make deeper connections to the relevance of the topic being explored. Integrating the essential learning into a theme creates an even deeper level of understanding where the students work with the concepts and skills in a variety of situations and across curriculum boundaries. Selecting the essential learning and enduring understanding is an important stage in the development and implementation of a thematic, cross-curricular course of study. The use of a model for planning, such as that of Wiggins and McTighe, Understanding by Design, provides the vital framework needed for selecting the skills and concepts that will be developed by the learner to ensure involvement, growth and success. Upon completion of the process, a formal, written plan is created that is used to guide both student and teacher throughout the course of study. Displaying the plan for all to share creates an environment of trust and commitment. Planning for learning should not be a secret and kept out of the view of the learner. Students need to understand the plan and see how it is designed to create an effective learning experience.

Hooking the Learner (Awareness) – Technology as a Tool

"Today's students – K through college – represent the first generations to grow up with this new technology.

They have spent their entire lives surrounded by and using computers, videogames, digital music players, video cams, cell phones, and all the other toys and tools of the digital age. Today's average college grads have spent less than 5,000 hours of their lives reading, but over 10,000 hours playing video games (not to mention 20,000 hours watching TV). Computer games, email, the Internet, cell phones and instant messaging are integral parts of their lives."

—Marc Prensky Digital Immigrants, Digital Natives

Engaging students in a learning experience can be a very complex undertaking if teachers ignore the fact that today's learners think and process information differently than in the past. Dr. Bruce D Perry, of Baylor College of Medicine, informs us that these differences in processing may be even deeper than we know because "different kinds of experiences lead to different brain structures." To fully connect learners to a new educational experience, teachers must present the initial concept in a way that "hooks" the students into the topic. This hook must have some element that appeals directly to the minds of today's learners. "Today we are going to learn about global warming, listen carefully because there will be a test on this at the end of the unit." Statements such as this are totally ineffective for motivating and engaging students today and even in the past. Our plugged in, technologically driven, game playing, text messaging, blog writing students of the 21st century will see such feeble attempts at engagement as lame and unworthy of their time, effort and attention. The hook must be personal, dynamic and relevant for the students and must appeal to their inner "light." We cannot expect students to become passionate and engaged when we are asking them to gear down. They want to be a part of the ride not sit back and watch the show. This does not imply that every lesson has to be a Cirque de Soleil performance accompanied by fireworks and technological explosions. It simply means that engaging today's learners requires attention to how they process information and what they see as personally worthy of their attention. Once the spark has been lit, the students will often set the forest on fire. It all begins with effectively hooking the learner into the experience.

Creating a Personal Passion

When students are engaged in their work and feel a deep connection to it, they begin to feel passionate about their learning. This passion results in a deep understanding and emotional attachment towards what they are exploring. You will see the students fully present at their studies, in the moment, in the flow. Learning takes on enthusiasm and an energy that is motivating and joyful. Students begin to see work as play and they will perform at higher levels than they imagined, often for the intrinsic reward of knowing that they are making a difference and growing as learners.

The key to creating passion is a simple formula that is based on meeting the needs of the learners. Students have both intellectual and emotional needs which are interrelated. For example, to engage the minds of students, attention must be given to fulfilling the three intellectual needs defined by Daniel Pink, achievement, autonomy and mastery. The same holds true for the emotional needs, which includes, purpose, intimacy and appreciation. To achieve passion for learning, the teacher must engage both the minds and hearts of the students. Engaged minds build performance and engaged hearts build passion.

Engaging the minds of students involves a deep understanding of the cognitive process. Knowing how students learn is vital to developing skills. Providing learning experiences that make connections and build on prior learning, combined with opportunities for sharing, reflecting, metacognition, critical thinking, problem solving and so on, continue to strengthen the minds of the learners. Effective feedback and evaluation strategies that focus on assessment for learning and allow students to show their knowledge in ways that are unique to them provide a solid foundation for learning and intellectual growth.

The heart represents the emotional side of the learners and is based on connections. Engaging the heart creates passion in students. Passion of the heart grows from the development of relationships, relationships with others and with the intimacy of their studies. The more students feel connected to what they are doing, the stronger the emotional attachment. A sense of ownership and purpose is created when students explore something that is uniquely of interest to them.

Independent research can be a valuable strategy for creating this passion within the theme or topic. Giving students the opportunity to explore an area of interest satisfies the intellectual needs (achievement, autonomy and mastery) as well as the emotional needs (purpose, intimacy and appreciation) of the learners. Attaching the requirements of the Independent Research assignment to the essential question provides the teacher with the "control" to keep the exploration within the curriculum boundaries. Although it may be necessary to "stretch" the area of research to meet the interests of the individual student, it is usually possible to make the curriculum connection viable for each learner.

Providing the Audience

When students get an opportunity to share their knowledge with others their understanding increases dramatically. Providing students with an audience gives them a reason for learning and a reason to do it well. Sharing their ideas and opinions through group discussions or during group presentations gives them the chance to clarify their understanding. Upon the completion of the Independent Research assignment students need to be given the opportunity to share their knowledge in an informal or formal presentation format. The use of blogs, podcasts, websites and so on are a few technological ways for students to share their understanding.

Allowing students to give workshop presentations or to make addresses during a symposium allows for deeper collaboration and communication among students. The specific format of the presentations should be decided collectively with the teacher and based on the students' strengths, learning styles and multiple intelligences. The more choices presented to the learners the better the students can display their understanding in a way that is truly unique to them. Power Point, Pecha Kucha (20 slides, 20 seconds each, power point presentations), Inspiration (computer concept map generator), dramatic presentations, models, artistic displays, song writing and so on, are just some of the many choices for students to use. Each presentation should have a minimum time limit and a mandatory oral component. All students should be responsible for creating their own evaluation rubric which is to be used by the teacher and peers. Metacognition and reflection are key components of the process and allow for growth in many areas.

Returning to the Essential Question

Throughout the entire unit, the essential question is the driving force. Everything that is explored, taught, analysed, discussed, presented and shared should be a reflection of the essential question(s). By doing so, the relevancy of the concepts will be reinforced and students are able to make the necessary connections for deeper understanding. Upon completion of the unit of study students should be required to answer the essential question. In doing so, the teacher will be in a position to monitor and formally assess the depth of their understanding.

Encouraging Action

Some students "get it" and are not satisfied to simply understand the main points behind the issue. Often these students feel empowered upon the completion then exploration of specific topics and demand an avenue for action. This is particularly true in the case of issues relating to social justice or the environment. They have a burning desire to take action, to have a voice, to lead others in addressing the problem and finding solutions. The role of the teacher becomes one of the enabler. The students want to drive the bus and the teacher needs to help the students plan a route. Many students when they get to this stage have a need to make a difference, a desire to be heard and internal burning to share. It is critical that teachers recognize this desire and guide the learners with finding options for their next step. Empowering students is the most powerful thing a teacher can do to reinforce the joy and wonder of learning.

Reflection

> "No more is there an excuse for letting knowledge accumulate in isolated puddles within students' minds."
>
> —David Perkins and Gavriel Salomon

As discussed in chapter five, metacognition and reflection are critical components of the learning process. "Thinking about knowing," "learning about thinking," "control of thinking," "knowing about knowing" and "thinking about thinking" are all phrases that help us form a picture of what metacognition is all about. Basically, metacognition is knowledge and control (Marzano, 1988). Students are successful when they are aware of, monitor and control their learning. The effective use of this skill involves focus and commitment to the task at hand "skill with will" (Paris and Cross, 1983). It is an attitude that acknowledges hard work and effort as reasons for success. Throughout the exploration of the thematic unit, students are required to reflect on what they have learned and to monitor their growth in the learning process. Exposing the learners to a variety of experiences such as drama, music, art, debate and role playing provides opportunities for students to develop their understanding. By employing a positive attitude and aligning "skill with will," students establish a strong understanding of themselves as learners and begin to form strategies to self-regulate their progress in the learning process.

A way for students to monitor their learning growth can be achieved by using an e-Portfolio. Electronic-Portfolios are personalized, online or offline collections of students' work that are chosen to represent their knowledge, skills and interests to diverse audiences. Developed over time, e-Portfolios show what the students have done throughout the program. E-Portfolio can include essays, presentations, research papers, images, videos, projects, reports, work samples, or metacognitions. The learners can also add personal thoughts and written reflections about the pieces of work included in the portfolios, and can invite feedback from others. This can help the students see their personal development over a period of time, as it provides a way to look back and reflect upon what has been accomplished. The e-Portfolio is a tool that gives students a sense of ownership and puts them at the centre of their learning process.

The Power of the Team – Collaboration, Team Skills, Communication

> "If everyone understands that each one is responsible for the performance of the team, then there is no place to hide."
>
> —Michael Oswald, Teamwork is an Individual Skill; Getting Your Work Done When Sharing Responsibility

At the heart of student centred learning is an environment that is supportive and fosters a sense of team in the minds of each student. Teamwork is not so much about a structure for accomplishing work, as it is a state of mind about how we accomplish our work. Webster's Collegiate Dictionary, 10th Edition characterizes team as being a "marked by devotion to teamwork rather than individual achievement." When creating a culture for learning that values creativity, critical thinking and collaboration, attention must be given to the development of a "we are in this together" learning culture. The creation of a positive, accepting, learning environment, where everyone feels valued and supported, is vital for the success of any learning that involves the student at the centre of the process. An atmosphere that encourages collaboration, sharing and growth provides the foundation for risk taking and self-exploration.

Creating a class identity or sense of team requires careful planning and effective teaching of skills. Skills such as positive interaction with peers, active listening, conflict resolution, problem solving and presenting an argument have to be formally addressed and reinforced throughout the program. Many opportunities should be given for the students to practice these "new" skills in a variety of situations.

Great Teachers Create Great Learning Experiences Resulting in Great Students

> "When you see a great teacher at work, you are seeing a work of art."
>
> —Geoffrey Canada, Education Reformer, Waiting for Superman

Ben Zander, conductor with the Boston Philharmonic Orchestra, had to confront a similar problem for over 25 years. He was frustrated with teaching students who were so filled with anxiety about the quality of their musical performances that it prevented them from taking creative risks. With his wife (Roz Stone Zander), they created a plan that would motivate and engage students in the creative process. Each student was given an "A" at the beginning of the course. The "A" was not intended to be a measure of their performance but rather an incentive to open the door of possibilities. To earn this final grade, the students were required to write an essay that would put them in the future. The report had to include the insights and milestones they had accomplished during the year of study as if those accomplishments were already complete. Although Zander made no reference to what happened to the students who did not reach their goals, the point being made was that when the barriers to success are removed possibilities become achievable. It is the teacher's responsibility to find ways to remove the barriers that block achievement. The giving of a "A" creates a mindset of anything being possible.

> "I had been conducting for nearly twenty years when it suddenly dawned on me that the conductor of an orchestra does not make a sound. His picture may appear on the cover of the CD in various dramatic poses, but his true power derives from his ability to

make other people powerful. I began to ask myself questions like 'What makes a group lively and engaged?' instead of 'How good am I?'"

—Benjamin Zander: Art of Possibility

Ben Zander applied his "new" way of thinking, the art of possibility, to his conducting and found himself less a dictator and more an "orchestrator of collaboration." His students openly discussed their creative interpretations of music, resulting in an environment of cooperation and engagement where both the performers and the conductor saw great improvements, not only in their playing skills, but in their creativity and emotional attachment to the music.

"Michelangelo... said in each piece of marble there is a beautiful statue. All you need is a hammer and a chisel just to get rid of the stone that is in the way of that beautiful statue. That is a theory of education! It's not the one we use."

—Benjamin Zander: Art of Possibility

Creating learning for students that is relevant, engaging and enduring is critical if we are to help our students join the 21st century with the skills and confidence that will help them navigate the waters of today and tomorrow. The teachers' role and desire to provide quality learning experiences for their students is the cement that holds the entire process together. It is their passion for learning, their endless desire to understand and to grow that gives hope to future generations. It is the teacher who sees the beautiful statue that lies beneath the surface of every student and does whatever needs to be done to help that statue form in both its internal and external beauty. It is the spirit and soul of every teacher that provides the shine, the spark that allows each student to see that everything is possible. Passion is contagious and once it is passed on, the possibilities are endless for both the teacher and student.

Conclusion

On April 20, 2010, an oil drilling rig named the Deepwater Horizon, sent a mayday call reporting an explosion in an area of the Gulf of Mexico. The demand for assistance signalled the beginning of the largest man-made environmental disaster in the history of the United States. The environmental, economic and political repercussions were felt around the globe. The spill stemmed from a sea floor oil gusher that was the result of the explosion on the Deepwater Horizon offshore drilling platform off the Louisiana coast. An estimated 15,000 to 100,000 barrels of oil leaked into the open water daily, resulting in an oil slick covering a 2500 square mile (6,500 square Km.) area. Experts were powerless to control the flow of oil into the ocean. Efforts were be made to contain the oil at the wellhead and to recover outward bound oil before it approached land. Finding solutions to the problem took too long. The actions of those responsible for the spill were inexcusable and the efforts by those to find quick remedies to the problem proved ineffective.

The ecological effects were enormous, killing wildlife and contaminating bays, estuaries and marshlands. It was feared that if the oil slick were to reach the Gulf Stream the sea currents would spread the oil into the Atlantic Ocean moving it northward to the east coast of the United States causing further ecological damage.

The hardest hit was the fishing industry resulting in economic disaster for those involved in seafood harvesting and related activities. By May 22, 2010 the oil slick had reached the fragile Louisiana coastline closing many oyster beds. Recreational fishing ceased affecting people in the tourism industries. Contaminated beaches, resulting in the cancellation of many vacations, brought about additional hardships for the people of the Gulf coast. A month later the effects of the spill were being felt along the Florida coast line. As of the middle of July, the problem had not been solved and the devastation continued.

Attempts to control the spill should have involved the collaboration of many people from around the world. Creative problem solving was required and quick action was needed to avert a catastrophe of an enormous magnitude. Finding solutions required a deep understanding of the factors involved. The effective use of critical thinking to develop strategies that would be successful needed to be employed quickly and efficiently. Those involved in finding solutions required the ability to work alongside others, to be accepting of the ideas and opinions of colleagues. There was a need to work across global divides. The "experts" should have been capable of accessing, analysing and seeing the significance of the data and information they were exploring. Our students/graduates need to be able to solve problems with more success than was demonstrated in this case.

There is a need for our educational systems to produce the type of learners who are capable of becoming responsible and productive citizens. The problems that face the world today require creative and collaborative solutions. Not only is it important for the world to have "experts" who have the skills to avert environmental disasters, it is equally valuable to have citizens who are aware of the need to rid the planet of our dependency on resources such as fossil fuels. The citizens of the world can no longer turn away from bad habits. Our planet is dying before our eyes and little is being done to stop it.

We are now 10 years into the 21st century. It has become apparent that citizens everywhere will need to be prepared to meet the challenges of the new global community. To be effective members of the world of employment, and to contribute as productive members of their communities, students must develop skills that will allow them to become actively involved in the world around them. The same skills that will provide success in the 21st century will also help develop good citizens. Unfortunately, there will be many difficult challenges and serious problems facing the world in the future. Environmental issues will continue to threaten our planet. We will require creative solutions to move us beyond our dependency on non-renewable resources. The global economy will present economic challenges for all workers. This will require an open awareness and acceptance of different cultural views. Technology is quickly changing the world of work, requiring employees to learn and relearn new skills on a regular basis.

The challenges are many. There is a need for citizens who are competent, engaged and responsible. What if our schools could develop life-long learners who see education as a path for growth and self-improvement? What if we stopped "manufacturing" learners and started developing reflective thinkers capable of making wise, informed decisions? What if our educators started teaching students using the new understanding of the way learning is acquired? What if we gave students the confidence to monitor their own learning and the opportunity to learn in ways that met their specific needs? What if we could instil in every learner the mindset that anything is possible through hard work? What if we created citizens who were creative problem solvers, capable of deep critical thinking, respectful of diverse opinions and secure in their relations with others? What if we could develop learners who were capable of working together to find solutions to future problems and who could provide alternatives to avoid such catastrophes?

I am excited at the possibilities of "What if?" I am terrified if we don't!

References

Armstrong, T. (2009). Multiple Intelligences in the Classroom. ASCD

Black, P, and Wiliam, D. (1998). Assessment and Classroom Learning: Assessment in Education. Phi Delta Kappan

Black, P, and Wiliam, D. (1998). Inside the Black Box: Raising Standards Through Classroom Assessment. Phi Delta Kappan

Boyer Report, (1998). Reinventing Undergraduate Education: A Blueprint for America's Research Universities, Stoney Brook State University, New York

Dewey, J (1997) (1910). How We Think, NY: Dover Publications

Dewey, J. (1916). Democracy and Education, NY: The Free Press

Dewey, J. (1934). Art as Experience, NY: The Berkeley Publishing Group

Dweck, C. (2006) Mindset: The New Psychology of Success, Random House

Fogg, J. (1997) The Greatest Networker in the World, Crown Publishing Group

Freire, P. (2000). Pedagogy of Freedom. Lanham, MD: Rowan & Little field Publishers

Friedman, T. (2007). The World is Flat, Vancouver BC: Douglas & McIntyre Ltd.

Gallimore, R. & Tharp, R. (2004). What a Coach Can Teach A Teacher 1975–2004: Reflections and Reanalysis of John Wooden's Teaching Practices. The Sport Psychologist

Gardner, H. (1993). Multiple Intelligences, NY: Basic Books, Perseus Book Group

Leven, T and Long, R. (1981). Effective Instruction. Washington, DC: Association for Supervision and Curriculum Development

Partnership for 21st Century Skills, (n.d.) A report and mile guide for 21st century skills. Washington DC: Author, Retrieved from http://www.21stcenturyskills.org

Pink, D. (2005). A Whole New Mind, NY: Riverhead Books, Penguin Group

Pink, D. (2010). Drive: The Surprising Truth About What Motivates Us, NY: Penguin Group

Prensky, M. (2002). Digital Natives, Digital Immigrants Part 1, On the Horizon, Vol. 9 No. 5

Pfeffer, J. And Sutton, R.I. (1999) The Knowing Gap, (Boston Ma: HBS Press)

Robinson, K. (2001) Out of Our Minds: Learning to be Creative, Capstone Publishing

SCANS Report, (1991). What Works in Schools, Washington DC: U.S. Department of Labor

Stevens, R. (1912). The question as a means of efficiency in instruction: A critical study of classroom practice, NY: Teachers College, Columbia University

Wagner, T. (2008). The Global Achievement Gap, NY: Basic Books, Perseus Book Group

White Paper Excellence in Schools. (1997) UK

Wiggins, G. And McTighe, J. (2001). Understanding By Design, Prentice Hall

Zander, B. And Zander, R. (2002). The Art of Possibility: Transforming Personal and Professional Life, Penguin Books

www.ingramcontent.com/pod-product-compliance
Lightning Source LLC
Chambersburg PA
CBHW020502100426
42813CB00030B/3084/J